rob 37 heroin - part two

rob 37 heroin - part two

robert j. kubiak jr.

CONTENTS

Introduction

For Mother's Day, 2022, I sent my mom a signed copy of *rob 37 heroin* (which my family did not know I was writing). I figured that since I published it just a month earlier, it would be a perfect gift. I thought she would find it interesting and insightful, and she would be super proud of me for getting it done. The book arrived at her house a day or two before Mother's Day and I called her that Sunday to wish her a Happy Mother's Day. Let's just say I did not get the reaction I expected.

"Happy Mother's Day!"

"Thank you. So, I read this book. [long pause] How many of these did you print?"

"It's everywhere, it's on like Amazon, you can get it online anywhere at like Barnes & Noble, Walmart, like thousands of places."

"Oh my God."

"What did you think?"

"Do you blame me for being a drug addict?"

I was shocked. "Is that what you got from reading the book?"

She paused a moment. "Well, do you think I should have done something differently? It sounds like you're saying your family caused you to be the way you were."

I was utterly surprised. "Not at all. You had nothing to do with the poor choices I made and the way I dealt with my feelings and tried to escape through drugs and alcohol."

"Well, I get that writing a book would be cathartic for you and you felt like you needed to get this out of you as part of your recovery or whatever, but what about the people who read this? What will they think? Did you need to publish a book?"

"Mom, I'm hoping it will help people, those struggling with addiction and their families and friends, and perhaps convince them not to give up on themselves or their loved ones. That if I went through 19 treatments before I recovered, maybe they can too. That it's never too late."

She was starting to understand the positive impact it could have. Then she said, "I don't know what I should even say to you, because it might end up in a book at some point."

I chuckled, but it made me realize something important. It showed me that there can be a giant disconnect between families and friends and the alcoholics and addicts themselves. I'm single and have no children, so my perspective was narrow and skewed. Perhaps because I'm involved in and around the recovery scene, and don't have to navigate with a significant other or kids or family daily, I assumed that everyone, including "normies" (people who are not alcoholics or addicts), would naturally understand and draw the same conclusions and make the same inferences from *rob 37 heroin* that I intended. It took this conversation with my mother to realize that this simply wasn't the case.

As we talked, we agreed that explaining and educating "normies" and those impacted by their family or friend's addictions was necessary. I asked her if I could describe our conversation in the introduction to this second book to kick-start this discussion and she was on board.

So, I want to say that for alcoholics and addicts, blaming our loved ones or friends or staying angry with them is not what's important. It can be important to acknowledge the past, but we don't sit around in 12-step or recovery meetings bashing our mothers and fathers or husbands or wives or children for our alcoholism or addiction. The "why" of the problem is not important. We need to figure out "what" we are going to do differently.

Alcoholism and addiction are essentially characterized by three things: (1) a mental obsession (it's all we can think about, getting the next drink or drug or whatever addiction we struggle with), (2) a physical allergy (once we start, we don't know if or when we will stop), and (3) an underlying spiritual malady. It's a disease. We don't ask cancer patients why they got cancer; we offer them help and treatment. The same is true in the recovery world.

Another point I want to make is that people come into recovery under many circumstances. The media has influenced us and when you think "alcoholic," you might picture a gruff-looking homeless guy drinking out of a brown paper bag under a bridge. When you think of a "drug addict," you might picture someone looking disheveled and stealing to get their next fix and getting high in an abandoned apartment complex (i.e., abando-minium or ban-do) smoking crack or shoving a needle in their arm. Turns out that's rarely the case. An alcoholic or addict may be a coworker, a friend, a family member, or a neighbor. They may be the person sitting next to you at a school PTA meeting or coaching your child's sports team – you simply don't know.

It's also true that addicts and alcoholics come to recovery after different versions of a "rock bottom" experience. The phrase "rock bottom" is thrown around a lot and people have different perspectives on what that looks like. Perhaps reading this right now, you do too. It's not the circumstantial "rock bottoms" that connect us. It's important to realize that you don't have to go to nineteen rehabs, have a few DUIs on your record, or lose your kids to DCFS to "qualify" for help. Maybe you just missed another one of your kid's soccer games that you promised you would attend, or you recognize that you're not paying enough attention to your family or friends and your mind is always elsewhere and you want to change that. That's what connects us in the recovery world. The emotional "rock bottoms," if you will.

The pitiful, incomprehensible demoralization that we experience until we finally can't take it anymore. That's what drives us to seek a solution. I recently heard someone describe 'despair' as being terrified that tomorrow and the next day, and the day after that, were going to be exactly like today. It was precisely where I was, and how many of us feel at the very end. The point where we can't take it anymore and pray not to wake up. It's when we finally surrender, put our hands up, and said, "Tell me what to do and I'll do it." We begin taking suggestions, remaining teachable, and are finally willing to get comfortable being uncomfortable. That's what it takes. Initially, it's not easy, but I promise it's worth it and it can be done.

I remember a quote from Simone de Beauvoir's *The Ethics of Ambiguity* that resonated with me enough that I scribbled it down in one of my notebooks: "With regard to the past, no further action is possible."

It's that simple. All we have is today. Sure, it's our dark past that can be our greatest asset in working with someone new to recovery. Sharing a little about it allows us to demonstrate that we understand. We get it. The need to escape. To suppress uncomfortable feelings. The pain. The isolation. The despair. Whatever it is. We don't regret the past nor wish to shut the door on it, and life is lived forwards but understood backward.

But the solution is the angle that we approach recovery from. Taking it one day at a time. Moving forward. Being present. Remaining in the moment and not ruminating or getting ourselves worked up or depressed about things that have already transpired. Nor do we want to future trip (aka disaster-bate) and get ourselves filled with anxiety about the 'what if's' and anxious about things that *might* happen. We try to focus on 'what is' and the present moment.

Nobody made us this way, caused this, or forced us into a life of addiction. It's nobody's fault. Whether you're an alcoholic, an addict, or a "normie," we are all nothing but a collection of the decisions and choices that we've made up to this point in our respective lives.

The fact is, we are all just one decision (good or bad) away from a completely different life.

The question is, what's it gonna be for you?

2

Point Break

Beating the proverbial drum with surreptitious allies
Conjuring up misguided passions regularly
Instincts have instinctively failed this lost soul.
Completely devoid of emotion –
Cornered by life.

Monday, September 13th, 1999. Gorgeous sunny day. I woke up and headed to Vilas Hall for my 9:00 a.m. Communication Arts class in Madison, Wisconsin, grabbing a honey oatmeal muffin from Jamie's bakery on the way. I decided today was the day. After the lecture, I headed back to my apartment. I grabbed a slice of cold pizza from the fridge, a garbage bag, and a large kitchen knife and headed to my bedroom. I locked the door and proceeded to slit my wrist.

Over the last month, I had descended rapidly into a personal hell and could not imagine a way forward. I exhausted every possible scenario and concluded that I wasn't physically or emotionally capable of navigating my life anymore. Suicide seemed to be the only option and here I was doing it.

I made jagged incisions and watched globs of coagulated burgundy blood ooze out. I cut until the initial trickle escalated and blood began spurting out at an alarming rate. Being the conscientious roommate that I was, I kept the garbage bag under my arm so the pools of blood wouldn't stain the carpet. Blood was pouring out, and I sat back and waited to bleed out and die peacefully alone in my bedroom with a VHS copy of Point Break playing on my small television. What a way to go out, watching a fucking Keanu Reeves and Patrick Swayze movie. Pretty fucking pathetic. After a minute, the bleeding slowed, so I squeezed my arm and the bleeding sped up again. I closed my eyes and waited to die, awash in perpetual nothingness. An hour passed.

I left no explanation, no note, nothing. My friends and family had no idea about the maddening despair and isolated hopelessness I had experienced for the last month. I heard my roommate on his computer in the other room, entirely unaware of the teenage tragedy unfolding on the other side of the wall. Unbeknownst to him, soon it would be toe-tag-time and he would have one less roommate to concern himself with. I drifted off.

When I opened my eyes, the credits were rolling on the movie. Carefully sliding over, holding the garbage bag under my bleeding wrist, I rewound the VHS tape and started it over again. I was literally in the middle of killing myself and I was concerned about starting the fucking movie again. Seriously? Clearly, I wasn't thinking straight. I laid back again with the bag under my arm, collecting endless amounts of blood, squeezing my wrist, bleeding out.

Another hour passed, and I was still alive. Fuck! My wrist was mangled but the blood was barely trickling out. Fuck! I picked up the knife and jabbed it into my wrist one last time. I don't know if I hit a vein or an artery or what, but a jolt of electricity shot through my entire body, and the knife fell out of my hand. It startled me enough that I couldn't pick the knife back up. I kept watching the blood but, again, after about 45 minutes, the trickle turned into almost nothing—blood was barely seeping out.

Then I realized I might not die. My apathy morphed into panic. The emotional Rolodex I'd compiled over my 19 years on this planet had no way to portray "failed suicide attempt." In all the movies I'd seen or television shows, someone would discover the person attempting suicide and call 911, and paramedics would come rushing in. Then the person either got saved or died. But I was stuck in a surreal reality that wasn't going either way. I couldn't decide what to do. My heart was racing, and I started to perspire. I was utterly fucking confused and quickly losing what was left of my mind.

Overwhelmed with anxiety and panic, I did the only thing I could think of and picked up the phone. I called home and asked my mother if she would be able to pick me up from O'Hare if I came home and she said sure, no problem. I cleaned up as best I could and wrapped mounds of bandages and gauze pads around my wrist. I threw on a long-sleeve shirt and fled my apartment. Before I ran into anyone who recognized me, I had to get away. I felt guilty and embarrassed and thought they would know what I had just done. I sprinted to the Memorial Union to catch the Van Galder bus that would get me to O'Hare airport.

I headed upstairs to purchase my discounted one-way student ticket. Keeping my head down, I nervously checked the oversized bandage on my wrist to make sure the blood wasn't seeping through, exposing my secret truth. I cautiously paid for my bus ticket and took every effort not to let the girl at the counter see my left wrist. I didn't make eye contact, because I was sure that if she saw the dilapidated disposition on my face, she would know that something terrible had transpired.

After grabbing my ticket and change, I said "au revoir" to the beautiful autumnal collegiate innocence that had been mine. I boarded the bus and took a seat near the rear. I tried to mentally prepare for a two-hour introspective nightmare with my eternal enemy—myself. I couldn't escape.

As the bus approached the drop-off location at O'Hare, I had no idea how I would explain my actions to anyone. I was not emotionally prepared to handle a situation of this magnitude and knew even less about what approach to take in confessing my dirty secret. I stepped off the bus, took a deep breath, and anxiously looked around. Behind the bus, my mother and father were waiting for me in my father's car. My first thought was, it's a weekday, why is my father here? Did he have the day off work? When I called my mom a few hours ago, I didn't imply that anything was wrong. I simply told her I needed to come home and confirmed that she would be available to pick me up.

Did she read between the lines, or have a mother's intuition? Did she summon my father home from work, sensing that something was horribly wrong with her first-born son? No, she couldn't have known, could she? If she knew, maybe I would get to the car and she would throw her arms around me and whisper, "I know. I'm sorry son but don't worry, everything is going to be alright." Then I wouldn't have the humiliation of telling my parents that I had tried to take my own life. I didn't know how they would react to this information. The entire trajectory of my life changed drastically and decisively the moment I hopped into the backseat of the car.

We pulled out and headed home. The mental preparations I had taken on the bus all presumed that my mom would be alone. I had thought about how to tell her about the suicide attempt a thousand times in the last couple of hours, but I hadn't expected my father to be there. I knew she would be shocked and demoralized, but I also knew she would be compassionate and would know exactly what to do—like she always did. My father was an entirely different story. He too would be shocked, but then he would be angry and humiliated by what I had done. He would be angry that his oldest son, his namesake, was a coward and a selfish asshole to pull a stunt like this while he was paying $20,000+ a year for college. He would feel that my actions destroyed the family's reputation. Nineteen years of his tough love and overly analytical guidance and this was the result? He wouldn't be able to separate the fact that I was a failure from the notion that he had failed in raising me. For the first time in his life, he would have to acknowledge the fact that he, for once, failed at something. That would be the most difficult pill for him to swallow. He would think about his three other sons and wonder, if this is what happened to the oldest, God only knows what might happen to the rest of them.

I sat in the backseat trying to visualize how this new scenario was going to go. Looking down at the bandages around my wrist I saw a faint red circle soaking through to the surface. I was getting warm and uncomfortable. Before I could convey the despair and hopelessness I was suffering from, my mother asked me what was wrong.

"When you called, it sounded like something was wrong. Aren't you supposed to be in class today? You're only two weeks into your Junior Year, what is it?"

I didn't know how to handle this, so I just launched in and said, "I tried to kill myself." I wanted to appear shaken up but, strangely, those feelings had dissipated somewhere between my apartment and my father's car. They didn't believe me. Maybe they didn't hear me correctly. I said it again and this time I also pulled up my left sleeve and showed her the haphazardly bandaged wound. Now they believed me. I didn't know how the fuck they were going to react, and I had no idea what facial expression I should display after dropping this bomb. Again, an expression for "failed suicide attempt" was not in my repertoire.

The next thing I knew, I was upstairs in the hall bathroom at my house in Barrington with my mom and I was peeling off the tape and bandages. I felt as though I was revealing ALL my fears and vulnerabilities to her. When I finally got everything unwrapped and my mother saw the multiple open, slashed, and jagged wounds, she realized the severity of the situation; a couple of Band-Aids would not do the job.

Parents don't get a handbook for raising a child. They do the best they can, but even if there was a handbook, it would be unlikely that it would include a chapter entitled, *"What to do after a failed suicide attempt by your child."* Nobody prepares for this situation and why would you? Never in your wildest dreams would you anticipate that, after a seemingly pleasant childhood and all the advantages that you provided, your child could be so overwhelmed with selfishness that he would do something like this "to us." The concept would seem crazy and nonsensical.

I looked at what was left of myself in the bathroom mirror and heard my mom talking to someone on the phone. My heart raced again. Who the fuck was she talking to? I *really* wanted to die at that point. I had imagined that only my parents would know about this, that we would resolve the situation quickly, and that I would return to school as if nothing had ever happened. Everything would just go back to normal. But as I stood there, I realized nothing would ever be the same again. And it wasn't. That's when things got chaotic—quick.

My mother hung up the phone and gave me the rundown on how we were supposed to proceed. The look on her face indicated that I probably would not be thrilled with the plan, but that it was a necessity.

"You most certainly need stitches, and the doctors will need to know what happened."

We weren't going to tell them the truth, right? We could just say I cut myself doing something in the kitchen on the blender or something. Or that some knife-wielding maniac attacked me, and they were defensive wounds. That could be plausible, couldn't it? But I realized that even the most incompetent emergency room doctor would immediately know what actually happened. In fact, they would likely be cursing me out under their breath for (1) doing this to myself and (2) waiting almost seven hours before bringing myself into the hospital. I reluctantly agreed to let my mom drive me to Good Shepherd Hospital and tell them what I had done.

The first thing I remember is being escorted to a small room by an ER nurse. She told us to wait for the doctor. Before she left, she meticulously locked every drawer and cabinet. This reinforced just how fucked-up my situation had become. I felt further alienated from whatever I imagined a "normal" person would be at my age. I would forever be known as the kid who tried to kill himself—but fucked it up. The nurse left, and I could see a police officer seated directly outside the door. I knew I would never measure up to the expectations that my father had for me. I was the oldest and was supposed to set the tone for my three younger brothers and this note was way off-key.

My mother was devastated. She asked me, "If I had a pill right now that would kill you, would you take it?"

Without hesitation, I said yes, and she knew I meant it. It was only then that my mother realized just how lost I truly was.

I was terrified of how the doctor was going to handle my situation. When he arrived, he did his best to stitch up the wounds and said, "Next time, come right into the ER when you're cut this bad instead of waiting so long."

I was like, "Next time?" What the fuck was this asshole implying? Looking back, I realize he was unaware of how the comment sounded, and I'm sure he meant no harm.

After somewhere between 16 and 26 stitches, I don't recall the exact number, the doctor told me to hang tight and that someone would be in shortly to speak with me. A few minutes later, a social worker entered and explained what was going to happen and how I should handle it. My worst fears were realized when I was told that because of the nature of the injury, I would have to remain in the hospital because I might still be a danger to myself or to others. I wasn't happy about this, but I thought, okay, so I've got to spend the night in an ER bed. Tomorrow morning, they would see that I wasn't crazy, a doctor would quickly evaluate me, and I'd be right back home. However, the social worker continued by describing the intake process to the "psychiatric ward."

Everything changed. This was not good. I did not need to be locked up with a bunch of crazy people in a psych unit; I said anything I could think of to talk my way out of this. My attempts were futile. Given the nature of my wounds, she said I would have to stay in the unit generally reserved for total nut jobs for at least 72 hours before I "might" be able to go home. No, no, I did not sign up for this shit. This wasn't happening to me. Things just kept getting worse and worse.

I was told that I could either sign myself in or they would forcibly sign me in, under protest, and the situation would be resolved in court. Okay fine, I thought, let's take this shit to court and let a judge say I'm not insane, just a confused 19-year-old. They would say I could go right home, and everything would be pizza and blowjobs. However, my mother broke it down to me—if they forcibly signed me in, it would become a public record and every future employer could potentially find out about it. It would follow me forever.

I stared at the form they were urging me to sign, admitting myself to the psych ward, and begged them to give me a third option because the first two were completely unsatisfactory. I was overwhelmed by this decision. I was clinically depressed and suicidal; how could I be expected to make this decision? If I had been under 18, I wouldn't have had to deal with this, and my mother would sign me in. I wouldn't have a choice and I would bitch and moan, but I would deal with it. This was the first real-life dilemma I faced as an adult. I signed the form and off I went.

They sat me in a wheelchair and rolled me through the ER and into a maze of hallways and double doors that automatically opened as you approached. I felt like an asshole being pushed in a wheelchair when I could easily walk, but they insisted. As we approached the secure entrance of the Adult Psychiatric Unit, my mother gave me one last hug and told me she would be there to visit and not to worry. "You'll be fine."

Easy for her to say. She wasn't being ushered into the depths of madness and insanity. I was only two hours away from Madison, Wisconsin, and the wonders of college life, but I felt like I was on another planet. I was so physically and emotionally exhausted that I wanted nothing more than to lay my head to bed and sleep away this nightmare.

It was late and none of the other patients in the unit were awake. It was good that I didn't have to deal with anyone, but I didn't have anyone to compare myself to, no way to gauge my level of fucked-up-ed-ness. I had no idea what to expect. After a never-ending stream of paperwork and signatures, they showed me to my room. It was the first room on the right, and I saw someone sleeping on the second bed near the window. I laid down in the first bed, balled myself up into a fetal position, and pulled the blankets over my head as if somehow that would protect all of my vulnerabilities. This very morning, I had hoped

I would never have to wake up for another day, but here I was, facing a tomorrow worse than I could have imagined. It took me a while to doze off, but eventually, I fell out and into an unfamiliar rehab slumber.

The sound of movement and random voices outside the room woke me up in the morning. I looked around and realized that the situation had not been a bad dream. I was terrified and very, very alone. I pretended to be asleep so they would let me be. I didn't know how things operated here, and I wasn't in any hurry to find out. My strategy worked for a while, and then every hour someone new would come in and try to start a conversation with me and/or coax me to get up and go into the "dayroom" and get something to eat. I hadn't eaten anything in 24 hours, I was starving, and I was thirsty as fuck. Still, I told everyone that I didn't want to talk and lied and said I wasn't hungry.

I wondered how long I could keep up this charade, and eventually, they stopped coming in and stopped trying to get me to get out of bed. I had wanted them to leave me alone, but now that they were, I wondered why they weren't paying attention to me. What if I tried to hurt myself again? I tried to kill myself yesterday, and I felt that made me somehow special. I wasn't a psychopath or a lazy-eyed psycho. I was depressed but I shouldn't have been there. I was just a 19-year-old kid who made a terrible mistake. I deserved special attention from everyone!

They continued to ignore me. I peered out of the room because I desperately needed to use the bathroom. But I figured this was some kind of psychological test, right? I couldn't give in first. They had to make the first move.

When the next person walked in, I asked where the bathroom was, even though I suspected it was right next to me in the room. I pretended like I just woke up. I slowly dragged myself up off the bed, still attempting to look hazy and confused while I fished for attention and went in to take a piss. As I was in the bathroom, I felt like I had won! They had succumbed to my attention-seeking behavior by coming back into my room to get me up.

I was so lost in my head that I honestly thought my thought process was on point. However, when I opened the bathroom door, expecting to have to finally engage with a staff member, I found them lying down on the other bed. I was like, this seems highly unprofessional. Are they so comfortable with their job security that they just decided to lay down and take a nap on the bed mid-shift?

I said "Hey," and was greeted with a hearty hello. The guy told me his name, which I immediately forgot. It wasn't until I noticed the socks he was wearing, with rubber traction grips on the bottom, that I realized he was a fellow patient. He appeared to be a forty-something-year-old man, and apparently, he was my roommate. I was embarrassed, but he was unaware of how I felt, so no worries. Then I realized that this presented me with an opportunity to ask a few questions to get the 4-1-1 on this place.

He told me this place was better than the other facilities he had been in. I wanted to stop him right there and be like, "Other facilities?" Frankly, I didn't want any information from a chronic, mentally ill forty-year-old. But I wanted to be quasi-agreeable, so I maintained eye contact and nodded so I wouldn't wake up in the middle of the night to find this unstable motherfucker choking me out or something worse. When he finished, I made my first excursion out of the room.

On the opposite side of the hallway was what appeared to be a nurse's station with a dry-erase board hung on the wall with patient names. I saw Robert K. and quickly scanned the rest of the board to estimate how many other patients were locked up in here with me. I counted about 12 names. Okay. I mentally prepared myself to venture further along and catch a glimpse of the eleven other characters currently calling this place home. For a moment, I hoped I knew one of them so I would feel more comfortable, but that thought was quickly replaced by fear. Wait, what if someone in here did know me? Then people would find out how I had fucked up. Then, when I realized that knowing someone here was unlikely, another fear appeared. I was not ready to talk to total strangers about my personal problems. I told myself that I didn't even have problems. I was here by mistake. I wasn't like "these people."

I came upon a woman quietly working on a puzzle at a small, round table against the wall. Hmm, I thought, she's probably catatonic. Then I thought, maybe not. Frankly, I wasn't even sure what catatonic meant, but I was still intent on labeling and diagnosing everyone in here with me. I was sure I was smarter than any of them. I walked right past her, and she didn't move or look up or say a word to me.

I saw an older man looking at a TV, but I didn't hear anything. Ok cool, I thought, at least they have a TV up in this place. I was like this guy must be experiencing audible hallucinations since he was watching TV without the volume turned up. BAM! Another diagnosis by Dr. Kubiak. Who needed a psychiatrist when I had all these people figured out in ten seconds flat?

I approached the U-shaped couch where he was sitting and grabbed a seat at the far-right end, far enough away so that if he went crazy, I would have a moment or two to get away. He didn't pay me any attention, and I scanned over the rest of the room but didn't see anyone else. I thought that was kind of strange because it was almost two in the afternoon. I looked over at the TV, then over at him, then back over at the TV, and said, "Want me to turn the volume up?"

I was trying to feel this guy out a bit, but he didn't respond. He didn't even look in my direction. Wow, perfect. I got up and walked up to the TV, reached for the volume button and I heard this guy say, "NO!"

I retracted my arm and looked at him, puzzled.

He said, "You can't turn the TV up."

I was like the fuck I can't, I'll do it right now. Shit, it would already be up if your messed-up ass didn't stop me! I gave him my best what-the-fuck face.

He picked up on my visual cue and said, "You can't have the volume on while the group is in session."

What? What group? There was no one out here but he and I and the silent woman working on the puzzle. Now I knew he was certifiably nuts! I started to sit back down, and he turned to me and said, "If you ever roll your eyes like that at me again, I will END you!"

What the fuck? He smiled at me and said, "I'm just fucking with you bro. We can't have the TV volume up because there's a group going on in the room right there."

Thank God. If he had pretended to come towards me before he explained he was fucking with me, I'm certain that I would have cried like a little bitch. I chuckled nervously as he introduced himself and again, forgot his name immediately.

"You must be Robert K."

"Yeah, I just got here."

He said he had been there for a few days and that it wasn't that bad. I was like, okay, cool. Then I asked what the group was about.

He said, "Fuck if I know, I never go."

Okay then, that works, group appears to be an optional activity. No problemo. A few minutes later the group let out, and I prepared to be inundated with introductions and questions. Okay, fire away people. But nobody paid me any mind. I was kind of insulted. I could see that I was the youngest patient there. I didn't know what to do and I'm sure I looked scared. Thank God a gentleman named Joe introduced himself to me and told me he was one of the counselors. He gave me the rundown on how things worked, but I was only interested in when I could talk to a psychiatrist so I could get out. He told me the doctor would be in around 7:00 p.m. Perfect. Sooner would have been nice, but that worked.

I wasn't sure what to do, so I went back to my room, laid on the bed, and waited to be discharged. At around 5:00 p.m., dinner arrived in the form of neatly compartmentalized trays containing a balanced meal representing all the food groups. It looked like shit, and I didn't know what the entrée was even supposed to be. I wasn't about to find out. And anyone who calls a mixed fruit cup a "dessert" is probably the same person that used to get beat up in school every day for reminding the teacher about the homework. I was disgusted with this nonsense.

I drank the four ounces of fruit punch, and a slightly stale bread roll and marched back to my room to continue awaiting my discharge. I lay there completely unsure of what time it was because the place didn't have clocks in the goddamn rooms! I was ungrateful and pissy about everything. Finally, someone appeared in the doorway and told me the doctor was there and was ready to see me.

I popped up and followed him into a small room where the psychiatrist was waiting for me. He left and closed the door behind him. I didn't know the procedure or how this was supposed to go. My only knowledge base was what I had seen in movies. I assumed I would talk, he'd ask some prying questions, and then after about 45 minutes, all would be well. I was wrong. I didn't understand the difference between a psychiatrist and a psychologist. Instead, he asked a handful of generalized questions, I responded, and the meeting was over in 10 minutes. Before he dismissed me, I asked when I could go home. He said, "Soon, but we can discuss that further tomorrow."

I was thinking, whoa, hold up, let's do this now playboy! But I said nothing and walked out, unsure exactly what the hell we had accomplished. The only positive thing about the meeting was that he believed me when I lied and said I didn't do drugs and only drank occasionally and not for over a month or so. I totally just pulled one over on the good doctor. I must be a born master of psychological warfare! Or maybe just another lying addict?

Okay, so I had to do another night in the mental ward. I could handle that. I wasn't thrilled about it, but after the shit I put my mother through, I owed it to her to stay calm and keep some level of composure. And my father? Well, I assumed he didn't understand me and most certainly thought I was a weak-willed pussy, so fuck him. I knew he hated me now for sure. I wondered why I had to wait until tomorrow to find out when I could leave, so I did what any mentally unstable addict would do and obsessed about all the possible reasons and scenarios which did nothing except accelerate feelings of anxiety and worry.

I plopped myself down on the empty couch in the dayroom with a look of great consternation on my face and stared off into space. An older gentleman in a goofy-ass Tommy Bahama-style shirt and boat shoes approached me and introduced himself. Great, another asshole with sub-par mental health here to brighten my shitty day. I didn't have the patience for this right now. He didn't say anything and didn't even appear to notice me, so I was fine, no worries. I figured he was too lost to pay me any attention. Then, out of the corner of my eye, I saw this guy toeing me up, so I looked over to him like, do something pops.

He remained calm and then out of the total fucking blue he said, "So you like popping Benzos?"

"Huh?"

He said, "You like taking Benzos? You like pills, right?"

"What the hell are you talking about?"

"I'm a counselor and we found Benzodiazepines in your system."

"No, you didn't," I said. "I don't even know what a Benzodiazep.... whatever the fuck you called it even is, so how would it be in my system?"

He started listing off a bunch of shit I'd never heard of—Xanax, Ativan, Klonopin, Lorazepam and I'm like, no, no, no, no, and then it occurred to me that maybe the ecstasy I had been doing regularly was cut with one of them, but I certainly wasn't going to tell him that. He continued listing the names of other Benzos and I heard him say Valium as well.

I thought, shit, I totally forgot I had popped a Valium a couple of days before, but I stuck with my, *"I don't even know what any of that stuff is"* routine. I was sure he knew I was lying, but he got up and walked away.

I thought, another win for Rob. They couldn't and wouldn't get a thing out of me—I was a steel trap regarding my drug usage. I didn't give a shit if the counselors knew, but at this early stage in my addiction, I was worried about my parents. I don't remember the finer details of the hospital stay because I was focused on other things, but there were specific instances like that encounter with the counselor that have stuck with me through the years. I had only taken Valium a few times in my life anyway, so it really didn't matter. I blew it off.

The next evening, I had an appointment set up with my psychiatrist and my mother. That made me a bit uneasy because my mom thought I was a wonderful child; she didn't know that I used drugs and I intended to keep it that way. She had never even caught me drinking in high school. If the shrink didn't blow my load, I'd be gravy. The meeting came and went, and it was perfect - drugs never even came up. But he said he was going to start me on a couple of prescription drugs, the names of which I had never heard before, but I was all for it. My head was fucked-up, and I enjoyed swallowing anything that might have even minimal mind-altering effects. Let's do this, I thought.

Then he said, "We'll see how you're doing for a couple of days on these medications before we send you home."

Again, I was not happy about it, but my primary concerns about my mom were avoided, so I would just put up with it. I spent the next two days ignoring everyone and everything; I took my meds as prescribed, and I set up appointments with a therapist and the psychiatrist on an outpatient basis for the following week. I was good to go, and I was finally allowed to go home.

I was so happy to leave the psych ward; I felt emancipated when they unlocked the reinforced steel door and let me out. Now I could finally concern myself with successfully ending my life. I played it cool and gave the impression that all was well and that I was excited to be home, even though my parents still had unanswered questions.

I enjoyed the amenities of being home. It was strange seeing my two youngest brothers scared shitless about what I might do when left to my own devices. But I was like, I'm all good, guys, no worries. They didn't believe me, but I didn't care because I was going bye-bye soon.

I had a few ideas on how to make my exit gracefully and after I met the mandated visits to my therapist, I planned to complete my second emancipation—this time from Earth. I had a handful of ideas and two requirements: (1) that it would be feasible and (2) that it would be painless. I was still debating whether to leave a note or something in the form of an explanation. Even though I didn't plan to be alive for another week, I tried to appear concerned about going back to school, so no one would be suspicious about my plans.

On the way back from the therapist's office, I stopped by my neighborhood Jewel-Osco and bought a pack of about 40 sleeping pills. I figured that would do the trick. I headed home as if everything was good and waited for the following day when I would be left alone. I was in such a hurry to take care of myself that I didn't write a letter; just popped all 40 pills and laid down on the couch in the basement and let a calm aura encapsulate me. I flipped on the television. One last glimpse of the world I was exiting and then I closed my eyes.

I didn't feel anything and didn't dream. Then, out of nowhere, I came crashing back to life. BAM! I looked around and saw a replica of my basement. No, wait, it actually was my basement. I was like, how the fuck did this backfire? How the hell did 40 sleeping pills (1) not kill me and (2) not even keep me asleep for five hours? I was so pathetic.

My depression was overshadowed by anger, shame, and embarrassment at being unable to finish myself. The only consolation was that nobody had to know about this and at least I'd get a good night's sleep. That was true; I didn't wake up for almost 18 hours when my mother shook my bed and told me to get up and come down and eat something. I could barely open my eyes, and I was unbelievably comfortable. I refused to budge, even after her repeated attempts.

She called the psychiatrist, thinking my depression had become so incapacitating that I had no energy and just kept on sleeping. Thinking he would help put a boost in me, he prescribed something, and my mom ran out to the pharmacy to pick it up. She returned and handed me a pill. I took it and then asked what it was. She said it was 10 mg of Ritalin. I couldn't fucking believe my luck, but I played dumb and asked what this might do. She said it would give me a little energy. No shit, I thought. I LOVED Ritalin. For the last couple of years, I snorted or swallowed them on a weekly basis. I even cut the cocaine I was selling with it, getting $80/gram, and people couldn't get enough of it. I knew 10 mg wasn't going to do much, but it did give me the energy to get moving a bit.

Everybody was happy for the moment. I hoped that my mother would give me the bottle, but she knew enough not to trust me. She left for work the next morning and told me she left my new pill on the counter with my two other medications. Damn! At least I got one. I took my pills, and my mind got going. I thought about everything and was entirely focused. And what did I focus on? Figuring out how to properly kill myself. I had been out of the psych ward for less than 72 hours and I had failed to end my life AGAIN, but I was determined. I didn't spend much time thinking before I decided on Plan C. I would kill myself by inhaling carbon monoxide from car exhaust.

I opened the garage and pulled my car in, closed the garage door, and rolled down the windows. I started the car and jerked off one last time. Then I waited to peacefully drift off to permanent slumber. Everything I had seen or heard about inhaling fumes led me to believe that you would eventually just fall asleep and would never wake up. I found out that wasn't exactly the case. It took quite some time for the garage to fill up with toxic gas, so periodically I would rev the engine to speed things along. Eventually, the air became more and more smoke-filled, and I was ready. I was all set. I felt faint, and I closed my eyes and leaned back.

And then boom! I started coughing uncontrollably, my eyes teared up, and my lungs felt like they were on fire. What the fuck? I could barely handle this. Why was this happening? I thought I was supposed to just fall asleep. I didn't sign up for this long, drawn-out cough fest with flaming lung pain and burning eyes—this definitely wasn't painless or quick. I didn't know what to do, but I did know that my tolerance for physical pain and discomfort was approximately equivalent to that of a six-year-old girl, so this wasn't going to work.

This was getting ridiculous! How long could I endure this before I would either pass out and die or pussy out? Like the little bitch I am, I couldn't take it and I turned off the ignition and ran back inside, coughing my ass off. I stood there hunched over for about five minutes before I could breathe normally again.

I opened the garage so the fumes could trickle out and I was so exhausted that I lay down for a half hour before I moved my car out of the garage. I returned it to its parking spot so nobody would know what I had attempted to do. I had been severely depressed and suicidal before, but now the feeling was magnified like 300%. The car in the garage was Plan C and I did not have a Plan D. I thought shooting myself would qualify as quick and painless (except for one painful moment), but I didn't have access to a firearm.

Now I was truly in a quandary. I had to do something I wasn't prepared to do, and that was to continue living. The mere thought of it terrified me—especially with the feelings of shame and failure after these botched attempts. The only consolation was that at least nobody knew about the last two tries. But I did, and I hated myself for it. I was still not only depressed, but now I would have to address the responsibilities of life and being alive.

Eventually, I went to bed as if nothing happened. I knew I would be left alone the next day. I prayed that miraculously, somehow, I would die in my sleep. Like maybe the sleeping pills from a few days before would mix with the fumes from the tailpipe, creating a lethal combination. It was a long shot, but perhaps it could happen.

I woke up the next morning and tried to come up with something to do. I hadn't done anything since going to the therapist the other day and had been told not to leave the house. While I thought about it, I took my morning Ritalin and that got me going again, and I thought I would go to Tower Records if that was cool with my mother. I called her and got the okay to go out for a while. Nice. I was feeling excellent off the one pill, but I would feel very excellent if I took seven more. I found the bottle my mother had hidden, and I swallowed five more and snorted two.

Then I was off. I was flying and it reminded me of a coke high, but I wanted an even more intense feeling. I stopped at a drugstore and grabbed a pack of Vivarin and a bottle of NoDoz. I wasn't sure how many I wanted to take but I was like, go big or go home. I took 16 Vivarin and eight NoDoz. By the time I got to Tower Records, I was geeked out of my mind and it felt amazing...at first.

After looking around for a while, my teeth hurt and I'm like, what the fuck? Then I realized my jaw was locked-up, so I tried opening my mouth to relieve the tension. It worked, but then my teeth began chattering. I closed my mouth and decided to deal with the teeth grinding because it seemed like the lesser of two evils. If other people saw my face quivering, they would have probably thought I had early-onset Parkinson's, or that I had been huffing glue before I came into the store.

As I kept browsing, I was becoming noticeably uncomfortable. I was wearing jeans and a hoodie and even though it was just 50 degrees out, I was sweating profusely. My brow got moist, and I could feel sweat trickling down my back. I got swamp ass. The whole nine.

I was holding a CD and a magazine, and thought, I better up jump the boogie before somebody noticed how fucked-up I was. I made my way to one of the registers with my jaw clenched and sweat pouring out all over my body. My hair was soaking wet. I couldn't stand still, and I swayed back and forth.

The dude's like, "Hey, you find everything all right?"

Look at me bro, does it look like I'm all right? But I said, "Yeah, fine."

He scanned my items and told me the total. He grabbed the bag and held it towards me. Taking a good look at me, he stopped dead in his tracks. Of course, that made me sweat even more. I was relatively sure that he thought I was a crackhead. He took mercy on me and left it alone and didn't say anything, but we both knew exactly what he was thinking. I fucking took my change and got the hell out of there. I hurried to my car; glad the ordeal was over with.

I took the CD out of the bag and tried to take the plastic wrapper off. But I was having a little trouble. My hands were shaking uncontrollably, and I was trembling a bit. It occurred to me that I had gone a little overboard with the stimulants, but I had a solid buzz going, so it wasn't entirely bad. I just had to get home, so I didn't suffer through another embarrassing encounter like that.

I popped in the latest release from Superchunk, *Come Pick Me Up*, and made my way back to the crib. I went down to the basement to watch television for a while. It was 10:45 a.m. and no one would be home until at least like 4:00 p.m. I was channel surfing and happened upon VH1 when the Red Hot Chili Peppers' *Behind the Music* started. I figure I'll peep it, if for nothing else, to hear them explain the true story behind *Under the Bridge,* their heroin ballad off *Blood, Sugar, Sex, Magic.*

With all the stimulants in my system, I had to work hard to focus on the program. With each passing minute, I felt more and more jacked up. I was uncomfortable, but I told myself it would pass, and I kept watching the show. I couldn't look away and was engulfed in the trials and tribulations of the Red Hot Chili Peppers. Eventually, I got jittery again and started sweating. My mind was racing, and my heart was beating approximately 100 mph. I hadn't eaten anything all day besides the pills, so I figured if I put something in my stomach, I would feel better and be able to relax.

I went upstairs to survey the contents of our pantry and see what might be at my disposal to calm my racing heart. I knew it would likely be difficult to eat much, so I grabbed four pretzel logs, something to drink, and headed back down to the basement to get back to the program. Each bite of the first pretzel made the pain in my jaw worse. It was painful to eat and even more difficult to force it down my throat. As much as I tried, I could only get three of them down.

I was completely immersed in the show and particularly interested in the downfall of their guitar virtuoso, John Frusciante. He, like most of the band, used dope every day, and it escalated to the point where they kicked him out of the band. This sent him spiraling further into his addiction and he turned up at a flat in Amsterdam, where he was interviewed by one of the filmmakers. He probably weighed less than 110 pounds and was ghastly pale. He was a disgusting shell of his former self and had a decidedly morbid life perspective. He honestly looked worse than any human being I had seen, and his conversation was so obviously skewed by his all-encompassing addiction that I literally felt his pain. It was the same pain and misery that I had been living with and that had been temporarily alleviated by the stimulants I ingested. I have never forgotten the image of him in his decrepit apartment.

Then I felt very ill, ran to the bathroom, and began vomiting. The pretzels came right back up and then I spat out what tasted like stomach acid. The vomiting progressed to dry heaving once everything came up. I was drenched in sweat and felt like maybe the 30+ pills I had taken might not have been the best idea. I hoped that was all the vomiting, but of course, it wasn't, and it just became more painful. It finally stopped, and then the phone rang.

It was about 4:15 p.m. and my mother had just gotten off work. She told me she was stopping to grab some food and that she'd be home in about an hour. There was no possible way that my stomach was going to be able to hold down an Italian beef and fries from Rosati's, and I wasn't the slightest bit hungry. I was trembling and the euphoric feeling I had initially felt from the stimulants had now escalated into a very unpleasant, speedy situation. My heart was popping out of my chest with each successive beat, and I wondered how long this was going to last and what the hell I could do to stop it. I felt sick again and kept throwing up stomach acid mixed with water.

My mom would be home shortly, and I had no idea how I was going to maintain anything resembling composure. If I couldn't calm down, she would know something was wrong, and I had no idea how I was going to explain myself. I thought maybe I would have a heart attack and that would have been just fine with me. There was just no way my mother would believe me if I said I was fine.

I heard the garage door open, and I handled it the way I typically handled these situations; I ran and hid in my room.

I heard my mom and brothers enter the house and my mom yelled, "Rob, we're home! Come down to eat."

"I'm okay. I'll eat later."

That didn't fly because my mother didn't trust me. I concluded there was no way around it—I had to deal with this.

Still sweaty and racy, I went down to the kitchen and said, "I think I need to go back to the hospital, mom."

"What? Why?"

"I think I seriously might have a heart attack."

She looked at me and said, "Why? What's going on?"

I was so worried and in so much pain that I told her everything about the pills and sweats and vomiting.

She still didn't know about my drug use, so she concluded that I had taken the pills to kill myself.

Fuck, here we go, I thought. I assured her that wasn't the reason, but she didn't believe me. God dammit.

I pleaded with my mother that I just wanted to feel good because I had been feeling depressed for so long, but she couldn't understand why I took so many pills. She didn't know that I had been doing cocaine 2-3 times a week for the last year and she insisted that if I wanted to go to the ER that she was going to make sure they re-admitted me to the psych unit. I was so nervous and sick that I thought, "whatever." I convinced myself that I could explain to the doctors that I just wanted to feel something because I had been feeling nothing for so long; that I had been just looking for a boost.

By the time we arrived, I was certain that I was going to have a heart attack and I wasn't thinking about anything else. They checked me out and said it would be several hours before my heartbeat would return to normal and I would feel better. I thought, damn, but whatever.

Then I learned that they were sending me back to the psych unit. Motherfucker. I couldn't explain my way out of this. I had to swallow my pride much like I had swallowed all those pills earlier, only the pills went down a lot easier. I felt like such a chump when I got back to the unit. By that time, it was around 9:00 p.m. and although I was feeling a little less speedy, there was no way I was going to be able to sleep. I begged them to give me something to calm me down and relieve my anxiety, but they refused. At around 10:30 p.m. I tried to lie down, but that was useless. They let me sit in the dayroom for a few hours and I went back to my room around 2:00 a.m. where I tossed and turned until breakfast.

By morning, I still felt ill and was unable to eat, but I was so exhausted that I finally dozed off for a while. I thought I was back in the psych unit erroneously, but I did recognize that I was still clinically depressed and suicidal, so perhaps it was a good thing. I was so confused I didn't know what to think. It had only been a week since I was released and I had no idea how long I might be in this time, but I assumed it would be a lot longer. I was right.

My father visited me when he was back home from work in Milwaukee for the weekend. It was either my first or second night and they made special arrangements to accommodate him because he couldn't make it in time for regular visiting hours. He arrived in a suit and a black overcoat. We sat down at a table near the nurse's station, and he had the goofiest look on his face. I was pleased to see how angry he was; I had finally pushed him over the edge, and it was like some sort of sweet revenge. All my life my father made sure that everyone knew he was in control and calling the shots and now for the first time it was my turn.

I smirked, and he said, "You think this is some kind of joke?"

I couldn't help it. I smiled back.

He waited until the smile disappeared from my face and out of nowhere, slammed both of his fists on the table and yelled, "SNAP OUT OF IT!"

I was stunned that he had lost his temper in a public place. Growing up, he took his anger out in private by using "the belt' on me and my brothers. For a long time, I had no way of understanding that he had completely fucked with my head and destroyed any sense of confidence and self-esteem that I might have otherwise had.

I didn't know how to react to his outburst. I sat silently. The counselors at the nurse's station asked if everything was okay and if I wanted him to leave.

"Yes."

I went to my room thinking, ha, how do you like me now?

My father's outburst demonstrated that he seemed to be incapable of acknowledging and accepting my mental illness. He honestly believed, and probably still does, that depression is bullshit and only for pussies who are too cowardly to deal with life. Seeing me in the psych ward must have annoyed the living shit out of him because, in his head, it must have meant he had failed as a father. I got a sick satisfaction in knowing that.

Meanwhile, my mother was doing homework on depression and was becoming educated and sympathetic to my situation. She probably blamed herself for allowing the abuse to occur while I was growing up, but I've never felt that way. It was not her fault. The only thing she ever did that sucked was to threaten to wash my mouth out with soap if she caught me cursing and one day, she caught me saying the "f-word." She grabbed my arm, pulled me into the bathroom, told me to open up, dumped three pumps of soft soap into my mouth, and told me to swallow it. I was caught totally off guard. I thought washing your mouth out with soap would involve bar soap, not liquid soap. Have you ever swallowed multiple pumps of liquid soap before? It is unbelievably fucking horrible. I could not get the taste out of my mouth no matter what I did, and it lasted for a day and a half. Okay, enough about eating soap.

Until this hospitalization, I was under the impression that other than my troubles, everything was kosher in the family. Looking back, I think this was the beginning of the end of my parent's marriage even though it wouldn't be finalized for another six years or so. I think this was the first incident that drove a tangible wedge between them.

The next day was extremely long and arduous. It was humiliating to see the same counselors from my first hospitalization. I'll never forget that experience. I was still miserable, but I was becoming sufficiently distracted by everything going on around me that I wasn't dwelling on my own shit quite as much. This was my strategy for the first day back. I wasn't looking forward to dealing with the psychiatrist and my main objective was still to make sure that no one figured out the extent of my drug usage. It was going to be a lot trickier this time around because of the circumstances surrounding my admission. But I was working on formulating a bullshit explanation that would explain away any doubts as to whether (1) taking all those uppers was a legitimate suicide attempt and (2) that I may have been doing more than just drinking and smoking a little weed at college.

I was exhausted by the time I met with the doctor and all I recall is that he greatly increased my medication and discontinued the Ritalin. When asked, I told him that yes, I was smoking a lot of pot up at school but explained that it had nothing to do with the severe depression or the reason I tried to off myself by slitting my wrist. It hadn't occurred to me that both times I was in the ER, they took urine samples. I thought I was being slick but quickly realized they already knew the truth.

I thought back to the last time I had taken ecstasy or did blow. It had been a couple of weeks, so I was pretty sure that they were already out of my system. I was worried about the Valium because I had no way to explain that away. But I didn't think that would be much of a problem because they were legal prescription drugs.

The next evening, my mom was scheduled to visit, and I agreed that we could meet with the doctor together. I didn't see any problem with that since my mom probably already knew I had "experimented" with marijuana. If the Benzos came up, I was going to say that a friend had given me something to help me relax, but I didn't know what it was. I also had a reasonable explanation for all the pills; I would say I was just trying to feel good again. I was as ready as I was ever going to be for our little psychiatric conference and felt a bit of relief by having my lies thoroughly prepared.

The next day I refrained from all the group activities as I had done every day so far. I was feeling less anti-life and thought that the psychotropic drugs the doctor prescribed might be working after all. My mom arrived a few minutes early and seemed to be handling things relatively well, considering everything I had put her through. I think she was trying not to appear upset, frustrated, or disappointed because she was afraid of sending me back over the edge.

Aside from my father, everyone seemed to be handling me with kid gloves. It seemed like nothing was expected from me other than to get better. I wished my life had been like that all along—low expectations and minimal pressure. It's not that I regretted being pushed because it helped me get through much of my life, but I wished that I could have taken a break from it when I felt overwhelmed. I still feel that way from time to time.

Anyway, after a quick chat with my mom, we met with the psychiatrist.

I was all set and said, "You guys know that I only took all those pills because I wanted to feel really good."

"Well Rob, why did you think you needed to take an excess of 30 stimulants to feel good?" the psychiatrist asked.

"I don't know, it just felt good, so I kept taking more."

"Do you think that was a healthy decision?"

I thought, that's a rhetorical question, right?

Then my mom took the empty box of sleeping pills and the NoDoz container out of her purse. I had simply thrown them under my bed, never thinking about it.

She said, "Can you tell me why you took all these sleeping pills?"

Oh shit. I was screwed.

I assumed that now they knew what I had been up to, and that terrified me. I mentally scrambled to figure out how to explain this away as well. But before I could open my mouth, the psychiatrist said, "Robert, if you're not completely honest with me, I'm going to have to keep you here much longer."

Damn, how to proceed? There was no way I was going to say, yeah, I've been doing cocaine and ecstasy in addition to the acid, mushrooms, weed, opium, hash, alcohol, and prescription drugs and yes, I tried killing myself twice while you were at work this week. I wasn't going to cop to anything that I felt they didn't already know about.

I wasn't sure where to start. I began with the easiest explanation about how taking all the Ritalin, NoDoz, and Vivarin was only because I wanted a boost and that it felt so good that I just kept taking them. I could tell neither of them believed me, but that was the closest thing to the truth they were going to hear from me—and if they didn't believe this, I knew it was going to be even more difficult to make them believe everything else.

My mom chimed in, "But what about the sleeping pills?"

"I got them so I could just sleep all day. I was ashamed about trying to kill myself. I just couldn't take it."

She gave me that, "You're full of shit" look that mothers have a way of doing when your lie isn't even remotely believable and before long, I copped to taking the pills to try to take myself out. They already knew I still wanted to be dead, so I didn't think this was a big deal.

Then she asked, "Why was there oil on the ground in the center of the garage?"

Well, I'd already said I tried to O.D. on pills, so it wasn't too hard to admit to the car in the garage incident as well. This was not going well.

The psychiatrist asked, "Your mother says you had a fun summer with your friends up in Madison; how did things get so bad that you thought the only solution was suicide?"

I tried another stab (poor word choice) at lying and said, "I lost my fake ID so I couldn't go out with my friends anymore and that's where it all started. I stopped smoking weed, too, and that's what brought all of this on."

I knew my depression was more complicated than that, but I was still so preoccupied with making sure my mom didn't find out about my actual drug use that I didn't care about getting better or killing myself. Protecting my addiction was the top priority. I didn't want to give the impression that my drug use had any correlation to my depression, even though I knew the two had to have gone hand-in-hand.

It was clear that my mom could not comprehend how my life could be so miserable that I would try to kill myself. How could I be depressed when my loved ones told me how much they cared about me?

I offered no explanation.

The psychiatrist asked my mom if she would excuse us so he could talk to me one-on-one. Of course, she agreed and left.

"Robert," he said, "I need you to be straight up with me and tell me what else you were doing. I know you had weed and Benzos in your system when you first came here."

I explained that a friend gave me something called "Valium" because I was depressed and that it helped me settle down.

"You weren't taking any hard drugs or any other pills?"

I sensed he thought I was lying, and I said, "Yes, I took Ritalin to help me study during school. I knew what taking them was going to do, and I just wanted that speedy feeling again."

That was half true, but I also liked taking Ritalin, as well as Adderall, recreationally. But he seemed to accept what I had told him as the truth. I thought that now that I was being much more honest, he would discharge me quicker. I was not thinking straight. When he told me that he'd check back with me in a few days and see how the medication was working, I knew what that meant. I was going to be here a while.

I said, "The meds are working great. I feel a lot better already." That was a blatant lie, but I needed to get out of the hospital so I could kill myself successfully at last. The combination of shame, depression, and anger was too much to bear and now I was getting blown off by this guy and I wasn't going to have another opportunity to harm myself for a while. I certainly wasn't going to try anything in the hospital because I might just end up getting stuck there even longer.

I walked out of the room pissed and looked to my mom for backup, but she wasn't having it. She didn't trust me to come home because she was terrified that I might do something stupid—and she was right. Honestly, I didn't even trust myself.

This was a major setback, and I realized I was going to have to enroll in the program and at least give the impression that I was working on getting better or I was never going to get out of this place. That meant I would have to start going to groups, getting up on time, and interacting with other patients and counselors. I wasn't particularly jazzed about it but at least I recognized what was expected of me.

The next day, I got up for breakfast and attended my first group. I didn't know what to expect and found it to be kind of fun. We played a word association game, and I was caught off guard and didn't understand how the fuck this was going to stop me from wanting not to live. But before I knew it, I found myself participating. There were only seven of us in the group, but we all were working together, and people were complimenting each other and seemed to be enjoying the exercise. We were engaged in a therapeutic exercise disguised as a game to keep the focus on the activity instead of the therapeutic benefits. The 45 minutes flew by, which was better than the way time crept by so slowly when I chose to lay in bed staring at the ceiling wondering what the fuck I was going to do.

I tried another group and another and soon I was going to every group just to remain occupied. I started to bond with these strangers and realized that they were struggling with some of the same issues that I was. My usual introverted nature was thinning out and I found myself actively initiating conversations with staff and patients. I gave some thought to what they were saying. My mind wasn't clouded, and I began thinking clearly.

One of the biggest reasons for this clarity was that I accepted the advice and encouragement of the counselors who told me that the only way to move forward was to accept and embrace the fact that I tried to kill myself. If I didn't accept the past, no forward action would be possible. Rather than feeling ashamed and secretive about it, I saw my mangled wrist as battle scars and focused on how I was doing in the present moment.

This realization didn't happen overnight, but it started to make sense. I started to believe there was something tragically cool about trying to off yourself. I envisioned myself as a tortured genius who was overwhelmed by life. Artists like me had a perpetual struggle so deep that the only escape was drugs and eventual death. This quasi-distorted perspective gave me newfound confidence and self-esteem the likes of which I had never had. I don't know if it was the medication or the meds and therapy, but the desire to die began to dissipate and I started feeling upbeat and somewhat well.

I got comfortable with the convalescent routine and stopped resisting things and instead embraced them. This place was safe and nobody and nothing could get to me and the problems facing me in the real world were temporarily put on hold. It was like taking an extended vacation from reality. I was in good spirits, and I felt stable. I started to care about various aspects of my life outside the hospital, and the staff and my family took that as significant progress and a positive change. I told everyone that I didn't think about hurting myself anymore, which was true this time. I knew my word didn't mean what it used to, but I could tell by their body language and disposition, which at one point radiated caution and concern, that they were now more relaxed and optimistic.

I'd been there about two-and-half weeks when I started coming around. I'd been on the medication for about a month, which was how long they said it would take for it to work. I felt good and made close bonds with a few of the other patients. I was attending groups, reading the newspaper every day, watching TV, and doing a lot of reading. My mom visited almost every day and even brought me carry-out from one of my favorite eateries, Schlotzsky's Deli.

I wanted to get out of the hospital now that I was "fixed," and move on with my newly invigorated life. The psychiatrist, on the other hand, wasn't as eager to discharge me. I understood his point of view because of what happened the last time they released me, but I kept pressing him about it, hoping he might speed things along.

There was also no push from my family for me to be released. My parents had arranged with UW-Madison for me to withdraw for the fall semester and return whenever I was ready. I would be living at home for a while after my release and my family was in no hurry to send me back to school. They trusted the doctor and if he told them that I wasn't ready, then I wasn't.

I still got the runaround on when I might go home, but since I was feeling better, I thought about returning to school at the end of January for the Spring semester. One evening I asked my mom about it, hoping to get advice, but that's not how it went down. She didn't think it was wise for me to hurry back to Madison, where I'd be left to my own devices.

"God only knows what might happen when we can't keep an eye on you," she said.

She was worried that I would fall back into my old routine, continue using drugs and alcohol, and get irrational again. They did not want a repeat performance of suicide attempts, and they did everything in their power to prevent it.

I told her this was unacceptable. I needed to get back ASAP. What was I gonna do once I got out of the hospital? Sit at home doing nothing until next fall? I argued that since they were paying the rent at my apartment, why would they just waste thousands of dollars when I could move back there? It made sense to me. I also didn't want to push my graduation back a full year.

My mom wisely just listened and then left it alone. "Give it some thought, and we'll talk about it again when I visit next time."

That didn't sit well and after she left, I told my side of the story to one of the counselors.

"Rob, your mom has a point. You've been through a major traumatic experience, and you shouldn't be rushing back."

"I'm not rushing back! I'll still have more than three months at home to relax and get over it."

"My experience tells me that it takes a lot of time to address all the thoughts, feelings, and behaviors that you exhibited. Treatment doesn't end once you feel a bit better; it's going to take long-term maintenance."

I was frustrated, but I already knew better than to ask the doctor again. He'd give me the same response. Normally I would have been anxious and obsessively worried about a situation like this, but I was feeling more subdued and patient. I accepted the situation for now. There wasn't anything I could do about it right then and there, and I figured that I had plenty of time to convince everybody otherwise. It would be a long time before I became familiar with the Serenity Prayer, but I was already beginning to accept the things I could not change. For the first time in my 19 years on this planet, I felt in control of my life. I had new confidence and self-esteem. I didn't know if it was the medication or if this was the "real" me because I had never known who I truly was. I liked this feeling and although I wasn't sure whether this was chemically induced (and I still wonder about it) I felt like I was operating at my optimal level and that I was able to truly realize my potential. It is funny how it wasn't until I lost my mind that I finally came to my senses. I was feeling great, and eventually, I agreed to take the entire year off from school.

After four weeks in the hospital, we were finally talking seriously about my discharge to a partial hospitalization program (PHP). I would live at home and report to an outpatient hospital Monday through Friday from 9 a.m. to 3 p.m. to attend group and counseling sessions. Initially, I would need to see a psychiatrist and a therapist once a week, then once every two weeks, and eventually just once a month. It sounded like a tall order, but it would get me back home and my weekends would be free. The only stipulation was that they wouldn't discharge me from the psych ward until I was successfully admitted into a PHP program.

They released me temporarily under my mother's supervision for an intake interview at Alexian Brothers Behavioral Health Hospital in Hoffman Estates. The doctors and counselors told me to act professionally and make a good impression so I would be accepted, but the advice was unnecessary; I desperately wanted to be discharged and I had my "A" game ready.

I hadn't been out in the world for a month, and I appreciated things in a way that I never had before. Everything from the sky and the clouds to the trees losing their leaves as autumn approached – it all seemed brighter and more real than they'd ever been. The interview, assessment, whatever you want to call it, came and went, and my mom returned me to the cozy confines of the psych ward to await their decision. I qualified. Fuck yes! I could finally return home. I said "ciao" to the other patients and staff and vowed never to return.

On the first day of the PHP program, I learned that being allowed home did not mean I had earned my parents' trust. My mother didn't trust me to drive on my own, so she arranged for me to be driven back and forth to the facility by a hospital driver in a cargo van. When I hopped in the van that first day, it was full of adolescents under 16 years old who were too young to drive. I was humiliated to be grouped with them. Things were not going the way I had anticipated, and I hadn't even arrived at the facility.

Alexian Brothers had two PHP adult programs; one for substance abuse and the other for depression and mental illness. The staff assigned me to the latter group, but I would also attend a handful of groups in the drug abuse unit. This assignment was, of course, based on the lies I told them during the interview—that I only drank occasionally and had merely experimented with marijuana.

The events of the day were familiar, having come directly from an inpatient program. I was, however, the youngest patient in the depression and mental illness program and the issues facing my associates ranged from severe eating disorders to clinical depression and obsessive-compulsive disorder; nothing I could relate to. At noon we had an hour break, and they served us lunch in the cafeteria. Before I knew it, the day was over, and I was back in the van on the way home. I was the next to last one to be dropped off and the constant bickering by the unstable kids and the two-and-a-half hours it took to make all the stops did not make me a happy camper. My parent's house was less than 20 minutes from the hospital and this chauffeuring scenario was not cool. I could deal with the program, but the van was ridiculous. I pleaded with my mother to let me drive to the program. She gave me the okay after a week.

Now everything was straight, and I felt human again. The freedom to drive was the last piece of the puzzle to regain control of my life. It was just a minor change in the grand scheme of things, but it propelled my spirits to an entirely new level. I'd never felt better in my life, and I looked forward to group sessions. I don't know if the sense of relief was because I'd felt depressed for so long or if it was something else, but either way, I was feeling so good that I didn't care. For the first time in my life, it felt like everything had fallen into place and I was free of all inhibitions. The only downside to being at home was that all my friends were still away at college and wouldn't be back home until winter break the third week of December.

I was acclimating well to the group therapy sessions, and I seemed to be in far better spirits than everyone else. At the time, I wasn't sure why, but looking back it makes sense because most of the other patients had serious problems, were missing work to be there, and had families to support. They were visibly stressed. In contrast, I had no responsibilities aside from getting there every day. I felt over-stimulated and energetic, and every day was fun and exciting.

Periodically, I attended substance abuse groups that ran concurrently with our program. I enjoyed those sessions much more than the mental health sessions and related to those patients much more. Honestly, I should have been attending the substance abuse track regularly and periodically going to a mental health group. I was liked and accepted by the other patients and made friends with some of them and hung out outside of the program – something I've continued to do up until now with mixed results.

The Alexian Brothers PHP was my introduction to recovery programs where the purpose is to get you to "recover" from your ailment or addiction by improving your mental health, relationships, and outlook. At this point, I had no interest in recovery; I planned to return to drugs as soon as I had the chance. I was just going through the motions and didn't pay much attention to what was being thrown at me. Thinking back, only three things come to mind.

One was someone saying, "If you want sympathy, look in the dictionary between "shit" and "syphilis," which I found incredibly amusing.

The second was a depressed, single accountant getting visibly annoyed by a young girl in our group and telling her in no uncertain terms that nothing she said mattered. He ended his tirade with, "Listen, honey, I've got socks that are older than you," dismissing her and everything she was struggling with.

The third was an innocuous side comment from a disgruntled middle-aged man to a girl in her late 20s who played the victim and whined, "Why do bad things always happen to me?" He cut her off in his best nasally impression of her and said, "Why me? Why me?' You sound like fucking Nancy Kerrigan—just shut up already." I laughed uncontrollably. She cried and left the room, and he got kicked out of the group.

So...yeah, that's literally all I've retained from treatment #1. Now, I totally get it when I come across a younger guy or girl in early recovery who thinks they know everything—that was me.

3

MADtown

Placating desires under expressionless skies
A crimson fog of effervescent delight
Bargaining with unseen certainties
Carefully circumventing complacency
Prancing untarnished through timeless tomorrows
Inspired harmony and an ode to new beginnings
Trivializing tedious truths with remarkable vigor
Forfeiting knowledge, yet unable to acknowledge
An unrealized new wealth of sagaciousness.

It was the fall of 2001 and my final semester of college at the University of Wisconsin-Madison. The idea to throw a little weekend party at our apartment started innocently enough. A few weeks after the airplane attacks of "9/11," there was a lot of pent-up tension permeating the campus. I figured a lot of people needed to get out and have fun.

Since I had delayed a year because of my suicide attempts and rehab, many of my friends, including my girlfriend, had graduated, but there was a handful of my core group of friends on the 5-year plan who were still on campus. I was on the 3.5-year plan because I had some AP credits from high school and took a heavy course load most semesters.

My apartment was located above a pizza joint called Casa Bianca on State Street in Madison. For those of you unfamiliar with State Street, it is the epicenter of nightlife, shopping, restaurants, head shops, etc. for the campus. The one-mile strip of commerce leads right up to the Capitol building. I was living with my buddies Charlie and Abel, and Abel was going to be out of town that weekend. We figured we'd get a shitload of hard alcohol, a keg, and enough pot to blind an ox. I'd set up my turntables and have someone come DJ and just tell people to swing through and bring their friends. I also planned on grabbing an eight-ball of coke for myself and my close friends. I had been doing the "marijuana and alcohol" maintenance thing since I got out of rehab, but with my girlfriend off at law school in Chicago and my closest friends graduating, I didn't have anyone watching over me. I figured I could get away with indulging in harder drugs again.

We kind of advertised to people on Thursday night at a bar down the street, The Angelic, that we were fittin' to have a big blowout on Saturday. One of my friends, Sam, pulled me aside and asked me if he thought there might be anyone that would want some ecstasy.

I said, "Absolutely."

"Okay, well, would it be cool if I gave you some rolls to sell, and then we could both make a few bucks?"

"Definitely, man, just let me know."

Now in my head, I'm thinking, I don't know, maybe he had 50 or 100 pills that he wanted me to help him get rid of. When he showed up on Saturday with a backpack and pulled out a huge bag with 800, I was like, holy fucking shit man!

"I don't know about moving weight man…"

"Yeah, it's all good. We'll just see what happens."

I thought we were just going to ask partygoers if they wanted to buy a roll or two; I didn't foresee moving quantity in the middle of a party. It's been 20 years now, but I believe our cost was somewhere in the $8-$11 range and, at that time, you could get $25 for a pill. Especially a nice, double-stacked, pressed pill as we had.

Being the savvy quasi-drug dealer he was, he said, "I'll just leave them with you if that's cool."

"Yeah man, that's straight."

Now, as much as I LOVED, and I mean LOVED ecstasy, the last couple of times I had rolled back in the Summer of 1999, when I took MDMA almost every day for three months straight, my body started rejecting it and I got violently ill. I'm talking about throwing up for 4-6 hours straight, dry heaving. It felt like someone was putting a drill through my skull and it was horrifying. I decided I wouldn't put myself through that shit again.

Then I had this great idea. I would make plenty of money by selling just a handful of pills and to get the party poppin' off I would offer any female a roll for free. I was never very good at the whole drug dealer thing and at that point in my life, I just peddled a little weed to friends so that I could smoke for free. I couldn't even manage to do that effectively. So yeah, this would turn out to be a very bad idea.

Things fell into place and what I had envisioned to be a little fiesta now had the potential to really blow up with a lot of people planning on sliding through. People began showing up around 9:30 p.m. and the flow continued right up until bar time at 2:00 a.m. I anticipated a big influx of people when the bars closed, especially once word got out that we had a shitload of ecstasy and girls were getting pills for free.

I headed to the back bedroom, Charlie's room, with a handful of my closer friends, and we took down some monster rails of cocaine. The way we were consuming the stuff, I imagined we were going to need more. So, my coked-up ass asked around to see if anyone could fetch us some more blow while I was drinking and handing out rolls.

I gave some guy I used to see up at the basketball courts, I assumed he was a townie, $150 to get us another eight-ball, and no surprise, he never came back. Another testament to my lack of drug-dealing and decision-making skills. The money didn't matter, but I knew at some point I'd be jonesin' for more coke like I always did.

We managed to make the coke last until just after bar time but at about 3:30 a.m. I realized we weren't going to find any more soon. I just said, "fuck it," and swallowed a roll and washed it down with a beer. At that point, all bets were off. My roll kicked in about 30 minutes later as things were dying down a bit. I was surrounded by a few friends and 10 people that I barely knew. I felt so good that I handed out rolls to anyone who wanted more. They were more than happy to keep the party going.

It's been 20 years and I don't remember all the details, but I do remember leaving for a little field trip with a gay hairdresser guy with blue hair who wanted to feed his puppy. He wanted to keep partying but didn't want to neglect his dog. He was out of his mind trying to drive and in less than a few miles, this dude straight rear-ends someone as we approached an intersection.

"Holy fuck."

My first instinct was to get out and run. Neither car had any visible damage, but if the police got called, I was totally happy to walk back to my place. Somehow this guy charmed the woman out of calling the police. He got back in the car, and we were back on our mission.

On the way back, we stopped at the record store adjacent to my apartment to grab some CDs because the DJ had stopped spinning records and we needed some music. Like a douchebag, I told them to send anyone who "wanted to party" over to my place and buzz the apartment. They looked at me like I was certifiably insane, and at that point, I basically was.

Eventually, we made it back to my place and only the true die-hards were still loitering around. Someone had a long wardrobe mirror laid out on the floor in the living room and they were snorting lines of ecstasy off it. A couple of people had ingested so many substances that they threw up and pushed through and wanted to stick around and keep getting fucked-up. None of us slept, and we continued like that for most of Sunday.

By Sunday evening, things started to wind down. Most everyone had been up for 36 hours or so. Charlie and I found ourselves with the apartment back to ourselves, and our epic little fiesta was finally over.

We smoked a blunt to wind down and get some rest. I took a quick shower and chilled on the couch. I attempted to count money from the ecstasy sales and take inventory of the remaining weed and pills. Someone buzzed, so we buzzed them in. I figured it was one of the usual suspects, good friends of ours, maybe Taryn or Mike, to hang out and smoke. But it turned out to be a couple of guys who I sometimes played basketball with at James Madison Park. I was in the middle of counting out approximately $8,000 cash, and I quickly shoved all that into my pocket. I didn't know these dudes well and, frankly, I wasn't sure why they were stopping by. At some point, I might have told them to come through. I wasn't sure.

They sat down and we smoked. Charlie played PlayStation 2 (PS2) with one of them.

The other dude, whose name escapes me, said, "I want to pick up an ounce of weed. Could you swing that?"

"Yeah, man, I could do that for $325."

"Cool."

I weighed out his ounce from the quarter pound I picked up a week or so prior and bagged it all up.

"I've only got hundreds. Do you have change?"

That's what he said, but he wasn't taking any bills out. I'm not exactly on point having been up for a day and a half straight, but I had enough sense to know something felt off about the situation. I also wondered whether he had caught a glimpse of the thousands of dollars I had shoved into my vest pocket.

Trying to be quick on my feet, I said, "Um, yeah, let me just grab change from my buddy down the hall."

Before I took a single step toward the door, the dude shoves a 9mm in my chest.

Fuuuuuuuuuccccckkkk.

He grabbed a large baggie, opened the cabinet, and threw all my weed and pills and stuff into it. Meanwhile, my roommate and this guy's partner were still playing NBA Jam on the PS2 unaware of what was going on just 15 feet away.

I took out my cell phone, not sure who I was going to call or what I was going to do. He snatched it away and yelled over to his buddy, "Yo, get the PlayStation."

Gun back in my chest, he says, "Gimme the money."

"What money?"

He unzipped my vest pockets and hit the fucking jackpot. He got the eight grand or so I'd stuffed in there.

I always envisioned that if I got held up at gunpoint, that, I don't know, I would lose control of my bodily functions or cry like a little bitch. But somehow, I said, "You are so fucked, man." I just kept telling him how fucked he was.

"Dude, you're fucked."

I couldn't believe I was talking shit to this guy robbing me who wasn't fucked. I was the one who was fucked. All the drugs had been fronted to me and he just took all my money. I don't know, maybe I thought I could scare him into stopping or something. It's tough to say, but I was not thinking clearly, and I was angry.

He even took the cordless phone handset, which, for those of you too young to recall ground-line phones, rendered it useless so we couldn't call anyone. His buddy had the PS2 and all the controllers and games, and they were out the door. He even left with a rented game from Blockbuster for the PS2.

"Holy shit. Did that just happen?"

"What the fuck just happened, man?"

We didn't know what to do. It's not like we could report it to the police.

"Yeah, Hi, um, two black guys just robbed me at gunpoint in my apartment and stole all of my illegal drugs and my PS2."

Good luck with that one.

Luckily, Charlie still had his cell phone. The only thing I could think to do was to call Sam. I didn't want to get into it over the phone, so I just asked him to come over. As we waited for him, the initial shock dissipated, and I was trembling. My heart was racing. Having been up for the past day and a half didn't help. I was a mess when we buzzed Sam up to tell him what just went down. He listened to the story and was a bit creased about the whole thing. We had sold cocaine together our sophomore year and he knew about my penchant for hard drugs. He knew that I had handed out rolls to people during the party, and he suspected that we were making up the story about the robbery.

I couldn't believe he had the audacity to imply that. Frankly, only about half of the stolen money was his and the other half was for some weed that my friend Joe had fronted me. That was another shitty phone call I would have to make.

The longer we ran through the details of what had happened, the more frustrated Sam became. He owed someone money for his end, and I knew that his primary concern was for himself, not his buddy getting jacked.

At some point, Charlie handed me his phone and told me it was my girlfriend, Shelli. She called him because I wasn't picking up my phone.

"What the fuck?" I whispered. "I can't talk to her now."

He insisted.

"I'm in no condition to properly explain what just happened and I can't handle talking to her now. Tell her I'll call her later, man."

"No man, just talk to her."

I sheepishly told her that some shit went down and that I was shaken up. She was furious but played the part of the concerned girlfriend and told me she was going to come up to Madison to check on me.

"You don't have to, babe."

"No, I'm coming."

"Okay."

Sam had heard enough. Knowing that my girlfriend was going to be coming up, he was a bit reassured. He didn't want me to leave Madison because God forbid, I left town without tracking down his money. What the fuck was I supposed to do? I was thoroughly exhausted, and I could barely think straight.

He told me that I was going to spend the night at his place so he could keep an eye on me. I didn't want to, but I was too spent to put up much of a fight. And I figured it would be good to just get the fuck out of there for the night. If anything I would be able to sleep easy, not worried about whether they might come back, and soak in the guilt I felt about subjecting Charlie to the events of that evening.

I threw a few things in a bag and off we went. It wasn't long before I crashed out. I remember waking up in the middle of the night for a moment and finding Sam sitting up, wide awake, watching something on TV with the volume turned down. He was an incredibly high-strung dude to begin with and I could tell he was trippin' out, worrying about things.

When I finally woke up, I slipped out and loitered around, waiting for Shelli to get into town. When we met, she was pissed off with me for veering away from my marijuana and alcohol maintenance plan. She had seen my struggles with hard drugs, and she was sincerely worried about me and whether I might be going off the rails again. It had been only a few months outside her watchful eye, and I had started dealing large quantities of drugs and had already gotten robbed.

We talked and, at some point, decided that the best thing to do was to get out of town. I would stay with her in Chicago for a while so I could sort out my life.

"You have to tell your parents."

"What? No way. Are you kidding me?" That was the absolute last thing I wanted to do. "I'm two months from graduation and who knows how they will react?"

I just wanted to go back to her place and get a better handle on everything. I just wanted to escape. I couldn't handle the consequences of my actions. I was a mess.

But I didn't just bounce back to being okay at her place the way I had hoped I would. I didn't want to go back to Madison so, after a while, I told my parents that I was back on drugs. They took it like you'd expect them to. They were shocked, pissed off, and ultimately disappointed. I had put them through a lot with the suicide attempts and rehab, and now this. I can only imagine what they were thinking, "Is this shit ever going to stop? Is there ever going to be a time that we don't have to worry about him?"

After a night at Shelli's, I ended up back home. I felt safe. I wanted to stay there forever and not have to think about everything hanging over me. But I also wanted to graduate, and I was missing an entire week of classes while I was holed up in the basement watching TV, trying to distract myself from everything. After a few days, my dad decided that this was not going to fly much longer. He took it upon himself to take me back to Madison. We were going to sort out the stuff with my teachers and the classes I missed and for the remainder of the school year, all I was to do during the week was to go to class and study and I would come home on the weekends. I think he also had a morbid curiosity about the details of the mess I had made.

What else was I going to do? I could have stayed with Shelli, but I wouldn't have graduated. I didn't want to finish my collegiate career at home at my parents' house, but I did want to finish out the semester and get the fuck out of Madison for good. After a week of being a shitless layabout at my parent's house, I headed back to school and tried to sort things out with my teachers and my classes and square things up with both Sam and Joe.

I knew Sam well, so I knew how to play that scenario. But I hadn't spoken to Joe. I'm sure he figured out through the grapevine what had happened, but there was no way I was going to be able to come up with the seven grand I owed him. I'm sure he was looking to hear Charlie's perspective.

My dad and I got back to Madison and you wanna talk about awkward and strange conversations? I had them. After each lecture, I approached the professor with the whole like, yeah, so last week I kind of got robbed at gunpoint and am pretty shaken up and I was hoping to make up for what I missed last week. They were more concerned and shocked than anything. I mean, Madison is a pretty safe area and there's very little violent crime on campus. That made this portion of the return process not too bad. They let me know that the Teacher's Assistant, or TA, would get me up to speed.

"Don't worry about it, just glad you're okay."

Okay, the academic side of things was cool.

At some point, my dad decided to spend the night at our place. Shitty, but whatever.

Next, I pinged Joe and, of course, he wanted to meet up. He asked me to meet him with a few friends at a bar up the block from my apartment around 9:00 p.m. Cool. I headed over and he was finishing up a game of pool and told me to order a beer, so I did.

When they finished the game, he joined me and said, "I wanna hear what happened, but I'd rather not do it in here, a public place, know what I mean?"

"Cool."

He says, "Let's go for a ride."

Fuck. Go for a ride? I got my dad at my place waiting on me. I'm still a little messed up by everything that happened and where were we going anyway?

"Not far, just a quick ride, bro."

I climbed into the back seat of a red, two-door Honda civic hatchback and felt trapped. Joe and his buddy took the front seats and we headed about a mile and a half away and pulled down a back alley. I fully expected to get killed, or at least get the shit kicked out of me. The car stopped and I freaked out.

"Why are we stopping, man? What's up?"

They burst out laughing.

"What's up with you, man? What did you think was going on?"

"Dude, I didn't know if you guys were gonna shoot me or tune me up. We're parked in a dimly lit back alley just off campus man, what do you expect me to think?"

They were still chuckling. "I just wanna make sure you're okay, man, and hear what happened and stuff. Don't worry about it, it's nothing. I'll cover it."

Joe must have been moving a serious amount of weight to be able to write off a $7,000 loss. Shit, he was doing pretty good for a young guy.

After my heart rate returned to something resembling normal BPMs, I laid out what had happened. They quickly realized there was no way to track these guys down.

"Fuck it. Wanna smoke a blunt?"

Yep.

Quick burn cruise later and we're back to the bar. We had a few drinks and then I headed home to an angry-as-fuck father trying to sleep on our ghetto-ass couch. I was supposed to be staying sober and finishing the semester and instead I had been gallivanting around getting drunk and high. Before I woke up, he left to go home. Nice. One less thing to worry about.

I started to get back in the swing of things, but I was still uneasy in my apartment and felt paranoid whenever I was downtown. I mentioned this to my friend Cassie, and she offered me a spot on her futon for Monday-Friday until the end of the semester. What a doll. I took her up on the offer, grabbed some things, and moved to her couch. Charlie and Abel were miffed that I had brought all this shit down on them and then dicked-out to stay somewhere else. They had a valid point, but I felt a lot safer a few blocks away at Cassie's.

As planned, I stayed in Chicago for the next few weekends. Things were getting back to status quo until I ran into Charlie on State Street on my way to Cassie's one night. His head was wrapped in a bandage, and he had a bruise on the side of his head.

"Whoooooaaa bro, what the fuck happened to you?"

He walked with me and explained, "I was at the apartment, and someone buzzed; I figured it was Taryn. I buzzed her in and unlocked the door. Then three dudes stormed in, all masked up with guns. They tied me up and searched our whole place and kept asking, 'Where're the drugs? Where's the drugs man?'"

Since I was out of the place and not selling, other than Charlie's personal stash, there were no drugs. After their first score at our place, they were pissed.

"Then they kicked me and roughed me up and shit."

HOLY SHIT! I couldn't believe it. Shit seemed so unreal.

"Then they ransacked the shit out of the place, throwing things everywhere and tearing the place apart. They stole duffle bags from the closet and basically anything that you could plug in or pawn, including the new PS2."

"Then what?"

"When they had everything, they just ran out. Eventually, I managed to get myself free and called the police."

"YOU DID WHAT?"

"Yeah, there weren't any drugs or anything and these dudes fucked our shit up, so I reported it as a robbery."

I wasn't sure I loved that idea, but it made sense and I couldn't be mad at him.

"Okay, are they going to investigate or something?"

"Well, yeah, they swiped all over for fingerprints and stuff."

I thought that was kind of funny.

"But the cops, man, they want to talk to you."

"But I wasn't there, and I haven't been staying there and I have nothing to say to them. Fuck that, I'm not talking to them."

"Well, when they were taking my statement, one of our neighbors walked by and asked me what happened. I told her that we had gotten robbed. And she says, 'Oh my god, again?' So now the cops are like, 'Whoa, whoa, whoa, what does she mean again?'"

She knew about it because, after the first robbery, we notified everyone in the building that we had been robbed and warned them not to blindly buzz anyone up; to make sure it was someone they knew, etc., etc.

"So, then I had to tell them about the first incident. I told them that you were selling ecstasy and weed."

"YOU WHAT?"

"Well fuck, man, I had to. I wasn't gonna lie to the fuckin' cops, bro. And yeah, I told them you weren't staying here anymore."

I couldn't fucking believe it. Why the fuck would he do that? That is straight bitch status is what I'm thinking, but at the same time, I'm slowly coming to grips with the fact that I caused all of this. Still, the last thing I needed right now was to get arrested or some shit. I freaked out.

"I can't believe you didn't know who it was and just left the door to the apartment unlocked."

"Dude, I'm the one that got tied up, robbed at gunpoint by three masked men, and roughed up! Don't go there!"

"You're right, you're right."

"Fuck man, I cleaned most of the shit up back at the place, but the cops have your new cell number and want to talk to you."

A minute later, after we smoked a bowl, he took off. I was tripping out a bit. Could I get arrested? What the fuck was going to happen?

Not too long after that, I got calls from a number I didn't know, and it was some detective telling me to call him back—that he just wanted to talk. The calls kept coming and I would cringe every time a voicemail was left. I was getting paranoid.

Eventually, he found out that I was staying with Cassie and would visit and buzz the apartment. I sat motionless, cautious not to make any noise. But other people would buzz him in, and I found his business cards slipped under the door with messages scribbled on the back, "rob – give me a call," "rob, call me asap, need to chat." I started leaving the apartment out of the back exit.

Every time I left for class, I was certain every car was an unmarked patrol car and that it would roll up next to me and tell me to get in and I would be fucked. I was miserable, and I thought he might even show up to one of my lectures and track me down that way. I breathed a huge sigh of relief when I boarded the Van Galder bus back to Chicago each weekend.

I was also paranoid about running into the dudes that held me up. I thought they might roll up on me, figuring I had resumed operations and set up shop elsewhere. It was not a pleasant way to spend my final months of college.

I didn't even walk at my graduation, worried that as a last-ditch effort, the detective might track me down in front of my entire family. Instead, I convinced my parents that attending the college graduation ceremony of their firstborn child was unnecessary. I didn't realize it, because I was too caught up in the consequences of my current predicament, but that would have been a tremendously proud moment and a happy memory for them. Despite everything, they had worked hard to get me through college. Years later, after I had done something to infuriate them, they reminded me of what a shitty thing it was to do. After shelling out tens of thousands of dollars in tuition and room and board, inviting them to graduation, and participating in it, was the least I could have done. That stuck with me, and I still feel bad about it.

Shortly before graduation, the guys who provided us with the rolls got caught up in a huge drug bust sting operation by the FBI and I was so grateful that I managed to get out of town once final exams ended. It was a far cry from the joy I felt my first day of college when my roommate John and I sparked up a joint in our kitchen after our parents left. "Welcome to college," he said. I never could have anticipated it ending this way. That was December of 2001 and I've still to this day never been back to Madison.

4

Botany Experiment

Transient auteurs peddling false pretenses
Decidedly ignorant and trudging along in a perpetual struggle
Alleviating innocent souls of the apathetic ambiguity of wisdom
Parlayed passions and recapitulated harmonies are divested
Extracting ornate and ominous vitalities quietly and quickly
Freebasing deception and distilling well-conceived cons
Taxing, tortured & treacherous.

After graduation, I moved back home with my parents. I worked miscellaneous retail and office jobs without much optimism or viable career prospects. After reading a book from Barnes & Noble, appropriately titled *Cocaine*, I decided it was time to start doing large amounts of cocaine again. As you can imagine, that went well. My friends called me "Blow Boy" and I was back on a tear.

About that time, my father had lung surgery or some shit. I don't know the specifics, but he was prescribed Percocet which he didn't take. I stole them one by one over the course of the next week. When my parent's realized this, they completely lost it. They had already given me at least 20 chances to redeem myself, so it wasn't a surprise that I was officially booted from the house.

Initially, it was cool—hotel rooms, mounds of coke, weed, pills, and alcohol. But after a week and a half, the money was gone, and shit got real. Life became completely unmanageable. I was homeless, sleeping under stairways in apartment buildings, 24-hr laundromats, a golf course, and a tree one night to get off the ground because it was snowing. Anywhere I could find until one night, around midnight, the cops found me asleep on the bench inside the Barrington Metra Station. They searched me and fortunately missed the gram of cocaine I had in an empty Parliament Lights box in my fleece. They took me to a homeless shelter in a church basement in Palatine.

The following day, some of the misfits and transients in the shelter informed me that we were at the church because of the PADS program. (PADS provides one-night stays in churches around the Chicago area for the homeless.) After that, I made the rounds of shelters, staying in church basements in Palatine, Arlington Heights, Barrington, Hoffman Estates, and Schaumburg, scrounging for cigarettes, and eating at the equivalent of makeshift soup kitchens. I spent Christmas with 40 of my homeless friends at the United Methodist Church.

On New Year's Day 2005, I inadvertently attended my first meeting of Alcoholics Anonymous at the First Step House in Des Plaines primarily just so I could get warm, and back then you could still smoke inside. I paid no attention to the program. After the AA meeting, the homeless community had been invited to a Greek Orthodox Church in Mt. Prospect. It was warm, they fed us, and we relaxed watching the college bowl games on television.

Toward the end of the afternoon, they also served us a slice of a ceremonial cake and said that one slice contained a nickel, and if you got the nickel, you would have good luck and prosperity the following year. Well, I got the lucky nickel and shortly thereafter, through a chance encounter with an Asian girl named Amy at the Arlington Heights train station, things started to turn around for me.

I got a good job working for one of the Big 4 accounting firms and paid a fellow homeless guy, to drive me to and from work in his car. I was still staying in church basements unbeknownst to my coworkers. After a while, I was able to get an apartment and a car. I was quickly ascending the ranks at work and things were looking good.

So, what do I do when everything is going smoothly for the first time in my adult life? I self-sabotage. Now that I had a few bucks in my pocket, I began selling large amounts of weed and started doing cocaine again. Meanwhile, my roommate decided to buy some grow lights and do a little botany experiment in his closet with some weed and seeds from poppy pods from Afghanistan given to us by our friend, Pennsylvania Reid.

I don't know why I felt compelled to get involved in all this at a time when things were going well—maybe I feared the responsibilities that come from success or anxieties or whatever, but to this day I've been unable to stop this periodic pattern of self-sabotaging behavior.

The status quo consisted of going to work during the week, smoking weed all evening, and just hanging out. Friends would come through to chill and smoke. I'd sell a little weed to whoever needed it, and then eventually they'd get going. Sometimes, we would have a few beers or drinks. Sometimes we'd smoke opium, snort Dilaudid or Morphine, or a little cocaine and some Benzo's here and there. Basically, whatever was around and whatever mood we were in.

One Thursday, we were doing a little cocaine and smoking some blunts, nothing out of the ordinary, but I didn't get much sleep that night. At about 6:00 a.m., I staggered out to my car on the street to make my way to work. I was relieved to find that I didn't get ticketed for overnight street parking. I started the car, lit up a Newport, and headed toward the stop sign up the street to bust a left and make my way to Euclid Avenue. Before I made it to the stop, three cars cut me off and entered through the exit to the apartment complex's parking lot. I thought, "What the fuck? That's kind of weird," but I rolled another 50 feet and stopped at the stop sign. I took a left and an unmarked, gray Crown Vic suddenly appeared behind me, threw on the whirlers, and pulled me over.

My head was still cloudy due to lack of sleep, but what the hell? I came to a complete stop, wondering why this guy was pulling me over. A dude dressed in full-blown tactical gear like he was ready to head into a riot appeared at my window.

"Put out the cigarette and GET OUT OF THE FUCKING CAR!"

Holy shit, this dude is serious.

He frisked me, "Do you have anything that's gonna poke me?"

"No."

"What do you have in the car?"

"What? Nothing."

"I'm not gonna find anything in the car?"

"No."

He searched the car, and I thought he might find some empty baggies in the center console. I was utterly confused; I still didn't know why I got pulled over or what gave him the right to rifle through my car. The next thing I know, I'm handcuffed and thrown in the back of his car. He took me to the Arlington Heights jail and threw me in a cell. No reading of my rights. No explanation—nothing.

What the hell is going on? I did nothing wrong. I had no weed or drugs of any kind in my car, so I figured I'm cool. Until about an hour later, when they brought my roommate in. He was also under arrest. Then I was concerned.

"Dude, what the fuck happened?"

"I was sleeping and the next thing I know I'm waking up to two guys in my bedroom with semi-automatics pointed at me, telling me to put my hands up. They drug me in my boxers into the living room and shoved me down on the couch. They said they had a warrant to search the premises, and they just started ransacking our apartment, bro. There were a bunch of dudes and a drug-sniffing dog. They kept asking me where the drugs were at."

What the fuck? A search warrant? A drug task force? A canine unit? This shit was serious.

"Yeah, they claimed they rang the doorbell and knocked, but I was sleeping so they straight up kicked our door in and came in all gangbusters."

They kicked our freaking door in? This is like some fucking TV show, FBI Files type shit. Holy fuck.

They took us from the large holding cell and put each of us into a separate cell. What was happening? How did they have a search warrant? Were we set up or did someone get busted and roll on us? Then I thought, I'm pretty sure no one read me my rights. Yeah, I'm going to get a lawyer and all these charges will be dropped because regardless of what they find or what we did, they didn't read my Miranda rights. I had watched enough TV shows and movies to know they have to read you your rights, right? The idea that somehow, I would magically get out of all this nonsense on some technicality gave me temporary relief. Man, I hadn't been in a jail cell since I got locked up back in 1999 for underage drinking and possession of alcohol, and that was nothing compared to what I was facing this time around.

Then I thought, don't I get to make a phone call? The next time an officer walked by, I asked, "Hey, can I make a phone call?"

He reluctantly answered, "You want to make a call?"

"Yes."

But then I didn't know who to call, and worse, I didn't know anybody's phone number. They were all stored on my phone. "Can I please get my cell phone so I can get a number out of it?"

"Sorry buddy, can't do that. Your phone's been taken into evidence."

FUCK.

"Did you still want to make that call?"

"Guess not."

Dude, this shit was serious. Were they going through my phone history? Would I ever get it back? What else did they take into evidence? Shit, I'm supposed to be at work right now. What was I going to do?

I sat down on the well-worn, lumpy, muted aqua-blue excuse for a mattress and tried to make sense of the situation and relax a bit.

It wasn't long before I saw an officer take my roommate out of his cell and head down the hall and out of sight. Where were they going? Where were they taking him? There was no clock, and I had no idea how long they were gone, but it must have been at least an hour or two before they brought him back. The cells were side by side so I couldn't see him, so I whispered, "Rob? Rob?"

"Yeah?"

"Where did you go, man?"

"They just asked me some questions."

Okay. I assumed they were going to talk to me and, yep, within a few minutes I was escorted upstairs, through a typical administrative office environment with people at desks working on computers, etc. They sat me down in a room with a couple of chairs and a table and shut the door. A plain-clothes Hispanic officer came in dressed like your average twenty-something-year-old pot smoker. He looked familiar, but I couldn't place him.

My mind was racing, and I was not sure how to proceed. I had never been questioned like this. My only frame of reference was from TV and movies. I figured I had two options. I could tell him I wanted my lawyer, which of course I didn't have, I barely had a driver's license at that point. Or I could answer his questions, provided they seemed reasonable, and I wasn't going to incriminate myself or anyone else.

He started off with, "We've got a northwest suburban drug task force with a search warrant going through your apartment. Where are the drugs?"

"Wait, why do you have a search warrant?"

"It doesn't matter. Just tell me where the drugs are."

"What drugs?"

His demeanor quickly changed when I didn't tell him anything.

"Shouldn't I talk to a lawyer?"

Another officer entered the room with a piece of paper and threw it on the table in front of me. It was a handwritten statement signed by my roommate detailing almost all of the criminal activity that we had been engaged in for the past year or two. What the fuck? He had listed every drug, prescription pill, and piece of dirt we'd been doing, as well as his little botany experiment in the closet. I distinctly remember that when he ran the idea of growing by me, I said, "That's fine man, but if anything ever goes down, you're gonna take the heat for every-thing." He had agreed, but that's not at all what his statement said. He acknowledged he was growing the plants, but he described how I (Rob K.) was selling weed, prescription pills, and opium. I couldn't believe what I was reading. He even included some things I wasn't selling but was just ingesting myself.

Epic deflate. Now what? Do I deny everything and say that it was all him? Even without his statement, it would be hard to explain why the quarter pound of weed they found in my closet was somehow his. At that point, I realized I was fucked. We could have tried to lawyer up and see what happened, but that option was out the window now. I didn't have many options. I could stonewall and ask for a lawyer, but then I would risk receiving a harsher sentence for not cooperating. They knew they had us. I had to play ball. They let me stew on my new reality for a minute and then continued the interrogation.

"Is what he says true?"

"Yeah, I guess, for the most part."

"Okay, so where are drugs?"

"There's a plastic box with like a quarter pound of weed in a shoulder bag on the floor in my closet."

"Yes, we got that. Where's the rest of it?"

"That's all I got."

"Bullshit, we're gonna find it and we are going to tear your place apart, so make it easy on yourself and tell us where it's at."

"That's it, honestly. I've got some personal stuff in the top drawer of my dresser, like another couple grams and some opium, but that's it."

They were expecting way more pot, and they seemed pissed.

I'm thinking to myself, I'm small-time, man. I rarely had more than a pound and just sold it to friends and a few people in my building. And it was just an eighth or a quarter here and maybe an ounce there, nothing like the kingpin type of lengths they were going through with a canine unit, task force, search warrants, and kicking our door in.

They don't do all that for a measly quarter pound, right? They were convinced that the tactical unit going through our apartment was going to turn up more drugs.

They left me in the room for about 45 minutes while they waited for the search to be completed. I was exhausted and put my head down and took a little nap while they were gone. When they came back, they asked me about a stolen laptop I had in my possession which had been taken into evidence. I explained that someone had traded it to me for an ounce of weed, and I answered a few questions about that. Frankly, I was surprised they didn't try to flip me or ask about my connections or anything.

They said we'd be done if I amended my roommate's signed statement and signed it. What did "done" mean?

"What's gonna happen if I sign this?"

"There will be an arraignment in front of a judge tomorrow morning at which point they will set bail."

Shit. We had confessed and were going to be spending the night in jail. On top of that, nobody knew I had been arrested, so there was a zero percent chance that anyone would be posting my bail. I was escorted back downstairs to my cell.

I tried to lay down, get comfortable on the cot, and sleep since we had another 19 hours or so until we'd be in front of the judge. Right around dusk, if I remember correctly, they came back to my cell and said they had some more questions for me. I was almost glad about it because it would get me out of the cell for a while. I figured this was when they'd try to lean on me for names or to try to get me to cooperate, but the conversation went a completely different route.

They explained that they knew I had been over to the apartments on Trace Drive in Buffalo Grove the previous night to pick up some pot.

Okay, great.

Then they said that shortly after I left, someone found an elderly couple who lived in that apartment complex had been stabbed to death.

Wait, what?

"We don't suspect you were involved or had anything to do with it. We know you were just picking up weed, but did you see anything suspicious?"

You've got to be kidding me. Could this day get any more fucked up? Now I was being questioned about a double homicide. This is crazy.

"We know you were buying pot over there and we just want to know if you saw anything strange?"

"Uh, no, not really. I don't think so. Wait, you know what, the entire time I was there, including when I was leaving, there was a suspicious black SUV with the lights off with the engine running sitting in the back corner of the lot. I don't know if that helps at all, but I do remember it being kind of strange."

"That was us. We were watching you."

Oh great. That's fucked up, man. An elderly couple was stabbed in the apartment building around the same time I was there. They said one of them was wheelchair-bound. Yep, things had gotten more fucked up.

I spent the night, tossing and turning trying to get some sleep. The morning couldn't come quickly enough. Eventually, an officer put a Styrofoam cup of coffee and a donut on the bar to my cell and said, "Time to wake up. We're gonna be heading over to the court in 20 minutes."

I was relieved that there was some action and was happy to get out of the cell. I had no idea what to expect when they brought us to court. They put us in a holding cell with several harder-looking dudes than ourselves. It didn't help that I had been on my way to work when I got picked up; I felt a bit overdressed in my sweater, button-up shirt, khakis, and dress shoes next to dudes in white tees and jeans with sneakers and tear-drop tattoos and shit.

They called us out together, and I scanned the courtroom and spotted my roommate's father in the back. Hmm, he must have used his phone call to call his dad. Sweet. Maybe he would post our bail and we'd get out right then and there. They parked us in front of the judge. I don't remember much of what happened or how the exchange with the judge went. I just remember it was going to be a $1,000 bail for each of us. After the bail was set, they whisked us back to a different holding cell where we sat until all the other cases were heard.

Periodically, a bailiff came in to inform someone they had posted bail and could leave. Every time the door opened, I prayed to hear our names. A couple of hours passed, and they left us with the other guys whose bail had not been posted. They lined us up, handcuffed us together, and loaded us on a bus to 26th and California, the location of Cook County Jail. Shit was starting to get real now. I had only heard stories about County, and I was certain that I was going to get fucked with or raped in the shower. I was certain it wasn't gonna be good. I did my best to hide how terrified I was.

We pulled up to the jail; they ushered us through a side door and down a maze of corridors into an area for processing. It had several large holding cells. We both ended up in the same cell, which eased a bit of my anxiety.

For some of these guys, it was like a freakin' family reunion. Dudes were dapping up and exchanging pleasantries and seemed to be "regulars," something we were certainly hoping to avoid. We absolutely stuck out as rookies to this scene, and I felt that someone was going to fuck with us sooner rather than later. Inevitably, someone asked us what we were in for, and we said that we got caught up for some weed. Manufacturing and distribution.

The dude asked, "Oh shit, do you stay way out in like Arlington Heights or some shit?"

"Yeah."

"Oh fuck, they told us you was coming and that they busted two white dudes out in the 'burbs with like 40 pounds of weed."

I only had like a quarter pound of weed at the house, but through the cops' corrupt, fucking gorilla math, they weighed the plants, the soil, and the pots they were in to come up with 40 pounds of marijuana so they could charge us with unlawful manufacturing and distribution. Rather than explain all that to these guys, we shrugged and said, "Yeah, it wasn't that much, but yeah, we were growing and selling a bit."

"A bit? Shiiiiiiit, man, I need to get yo digits."

We were getting serious street cred in the holding cell, and we were happy to roll with it. I figured they would be less likely to fuck with us if they considered us legit and moving a lot of weight.

They moved us along from holding cell to holding cell as they processed the guys ahead of us. When we got to the third cell, they called my name, and I surrendered my clothes and possessions in exchange for a lovely little khaki outfit. Then they sent me through to see the 'dick doctor'.

Yeah man, back then they were doing dick-pricks. Without consent, they jammed a Q-Tip into the tip of your dick as an STD test. A few years later there would be a class action lawsuit about that and had I mailed back the letter they sent, I think I ultimately could have gotten a check for a few hundred bucks.

After we changed into our new get-up and endured the dick-prick, we went around a counter, and they took our picture. That was the last step in processing. We were put back in a cell and waited to be assigned to a unit. The guards handling this process enjoyed fucking with us. One white dude with an Irish flag tattoo on his forearm told me how fucked I was and that he was going to buy my Cadillac at auction for next to nothing. I did not appreciate it.

Fun Fact: Two years later, I ran into a guy by the name of Frank in rehab at Holy Family Keys to Recovery in Des Plaines. Once I saw his tattoo, I knew he was the same guy from County. Turned out he had a drinking problem, and I couldn't resist reminding him of our encounter. In front of the patients, I rehashed the incident and told him he was a prick for fucking with me during processing.

"Yeah, well, I was drinking pretty heavily around that time," he said. Small fuckin' world, right?

Before the assignment, they did another call of people who had posted bail. They called my roommate, and I expected to hear my name, but it didn't happen. What the fuck man? I did not feel good watching him leave and being left in a cramped cell with at least 45 unruly convicts who were getting restless. Fuck man, looks like I'm doing this alone. Eventually, they took me upstairs with a group of guys to get stripped searched, and do the whole spread your cheeks and cough routine. Again, the guards berated us and again, they put us in another holding cell.

This process was not what one would describe as streamlined and efficient. The routine took over six hours, and I had yet to get to my unit. Before I was assigned, they called my name along with a few others and told us, "You made bail." Oh my god, thank fucking god man. I don't know who paid my bail, but the obvious assumption was my roommate's dad. But why didn't he fucking bail me out at the same time as him? It didn't matter, I felt as much relief at that moment as I generally did getting high.

Even the process of releasing you was crazy slow, and it took almost two hours. I walked out, putting on my belt and fishing through my belongings for a Newport. I looked around to see who bailed me out, but nobody was there, just a few stragglers from the neighborhood looking to bum squares. After waiting about 20 minutes, I walked over to one of the cab drivers parked outside and asked if he would take me to the suburbs. He wanted a flat rate of $45. Done. Let's ride.

I expected to find my roommate back at the apartment, but nobody was there. Our place was destroyed. Soil was strewn everywhere, the cabinets were open, every pillow on the couch and chairs was upended, and my mattress was on the floor along with most of the clothes from my closet. The front door was jacked up and wedged closed after they kicked it in. You couldn't have fucked our place more if you tried. The real surprise was that they left 4-5 solid-size blunt roaches in the ashtrays.

My cell phone was still in evidence, and I didn't know what was going on with my roommate or who had bailed me out. A random neighbor from across the courtyard stopped over with some Hamburger Helper he made for me. Fuckin' weird, right? I was happy to take it and re-hash the story of what went down.

"Do you know who rolled on you?"

"I don't know, man."

Not long after that, my roommate returned with his dad to see if I had made it home. He said they knew from his own experience that it would take hours for me to get through the release process, and they went and grabbed some food. They must have come back right after I left. I thanked his dad and promised to pay him back. I didn't live up to that promise for four years, but eventually, he got that thousand back from me.

We chatted a bit and then I dragged my mattress back onto my bed. I desperately needed to get some sleep. I was so glad to be back home.

Fast forward a few months, we lawyered up and got off with a slap on the wrist. We pled guilty. I mean, there was no denying anything at that point, and they gave us two years of 710 felony probation. This required 30 hours of community service, drug and alcohol evaluations, and court fees. It was nothing in the grand scheme of things and if we completed the probation successfully, we would not have a conviction on our record. This was the first time my usage and lifestyle resulted in legal issues, but for some reason, I was able to hang on to my job. I told myself that things were still manageable.

In my head, I equated having a job with "my life is still under control." This theme continued throughout the course of my addiction. I thought that if I was bringing finances in, or had a place crash at night, that I'd figure it out and somehow land on my feet.

All I had to do was not smoke pot and do drugs for the next two years. I lasted maybe a month. I went to the first probation appointment and wasn't drug tested, so I thought, fuck this. The whole sobriety thing was killing me, man. I needed my "medicine" to get right. After a few months, we were back to the same lifestyle as before the arrest, except that I stopped selling weed and my roommate ceased his little biophilic fun in his closet.

It wasn't until the ninth month of my probation that I finally got dropped, and I knew I was going to come up dirty for weed when I came back the following month. As a testament to the power of this disease, I showed up at the courthouse coked up out of mind and all jittery and anxious. Who the fuck does that? I was paranoid enough as it was, but entering a building full of cops and probation officers was not where your average cocaine user likes to find themselves.

"Robert, you tested positive."

Yep.

"You'll have to appear before the judge next month for a hearing at which point, he'll decide whether to terminate your probation."

If he did, I would have a felony on my record. If he gave me a second chance and declared that I had violated the terms of probation, the requirements would become more intense and demanding and, of course, I would have to pay more legal fees and court costs.

I consulted with my lawyer, and he told me to expect that the judge would violate me and that I would have to pay $2,500 or get sent back to Cook County. Fuck. I didn't have that kind of money. The most I could get would be a thousand, so I found an acquaintance of mine who peddled his fair share of weed to pick up the slack for the fee. I made him agree to crash at my apartment that night to make sure he would be in court to post my bail so I wouldn't have to take the bus down to 26th and California again. Of course, he went out gallivanting and bar-hopping the night before and showed up around 2 a.m. Whatever, I thought, at least he's here.

At 8:30 a.m., it was time to go to court, but he wouldn't get up. Dude, what the fuck, man? I begged him to come with me. He told me to chill and that he would meet me there in 45 minutes for the 9:30 a.m. hearing.

Long story short, the cocksucker blew me off and I couldn't pay bail and off we go on another vacation down to County. Same routine, hours going through processing, dick prick, the whole nine, but this time I'm not bailed out and get assigned to my unit and cell block.

I thought I was going to be locked in a cell with another guy like you see on TV and in movies, but that was not the case. Picture a huge room with high ceilings and about 250 sets of bunk beds split in the middle. A handful of lunch tables with bright fluorescent lights on one end and television sets affixed to the ceiling in each corner of the room playing shitty Hallmark Christmas movies 24-7 because I arrived on December 22nd.

I was one of only 20 or so Caucasians in the entire place. They assigned me to the top bunk amidst the sea of bunk beds. The bed was so incredibly high that you had to step on the railings or hold on to the bed next to you to hoist yourself up. I didn't mind because it felt safer being up top rather than close to the ground where you were more exposed.

It felt like all eyes were on me. I didn't know the routine or what we were supposed to do. Did we have to take showers? Did they take us to the "yard" and give us recreation time? Probably not, as it was the middle of the winter. I didn't know what to do other than lounge around on my bunk and try not to piss anyone off.

After a while, it became clear that this was a big holding pen for guys that had upcoming court dates and couldn't post bail, for one reason or another. Surprisingly, it seemed pretty low-key and chill. There wasn't any drama or arguments or anything like that, but I remained uneasy. I didn't know if the guys around me were in for petty drug possession crimes or aggravated assault or murder or something. I kept my head down and stayed in my lane.

I had no idea how long I would be there. I prayed that someone would post my bail. A couple of days went by and nothing. Then one evening my name was called along with a host of others and we were told to line up. Thank God, man. It's time to get the fuck outta here.

They rounded up about 20 or so guys, and marched us down to the depths of antiquity in Cook County Jail to a place the regulars affectionately refer to as "water world." It was the kitchen for the entire prison and where they prepped the food. We were told that we would be responsible for cleaning every single pot, pan, tray, etc. that had been used by the entire prison that day. We would also clean the machines, wash everything down, and mop the floor.

Shit took us at least six hours from start to finish. There were no breaks and if you tried to rest, you would have a guard in your face warning you to keep working. By the time we finished, it was around

3:00 a.m. and we were covered in sweat and soaking wet from the cleaning sprayers. They marched us back up into the blindingly bright fluorescent lights of the dorm. It was so bright that it was next to impossible to sleep. I couldn't sleep anyway because of the television noise and random dudes loitering about, playing spades and shit. It was fucking miserable.

I was fine the first two days and nights, but I was not down with this manual labor bullshit. The following evening, my name was called for a second time, and I gathered from eavesdropping that you worked three days and then had four days off. Muthafucker man. The second evening down in water world, I couldn't take it anymore. My court date wasn't for another month, and I hadn't showered for a few days. I was exhausted and sweaty and cold at the same time. I was five minutes from laying my broom down and telling the guards, look man, I'm done. Throw me in solitary, do whatever you need to, but I'm done with this shit. I was at my breaking point. And right before I did it, at about midnight, my name was called along with 4-5 other guys. The guards told us that we made bail.

Holy shit, A-*fucking*-MEN.

It was just as slow as the first time and took almost two hours for them to process us out. Then, when I got my possessions back, the $160 I had in cash was gone. They stole it. That was all the money I had left. I waltzed out the front door just after 2:00 a.m. on Christmas morning. It was easily the best Christmas gift I had ever received.

The paperwork said my bail was posted by the buddy that ghosted me the day of my court date. I wasn't concerned that he waited three days to post my bail, but I didn't know how the fuck I was going to get home. I had maybe $8 in my bank account, and I was a long way from Arlington Heights.

I debated what to do over a couple of Newport's. Then I asked a cabbie if he'd drive me on a flat rate and he agreed to $45. I couldn't pay the guy, but I figured my roommate could float me some money, and if not, somehow, I'd have to lose this guy or just take off running or some shit. Lucky for me when I got home, my roommate and the dude that posted my bail were there, and they tossed me $55 to give to the cabbie.

We smoked a blunt, exchanged Merry Christmas pleasantries, and headed to Denny's to get some food. I hadn't eaten much of anything in the past four days, deciding to forgo 90% of the slop they fed us at County. I am an extremely picky eater to begin with and that food was horrible.

After my little vacation back to County, I busted ass to finish the community service, fines, and everything else required for my probation to end. I was not trying to head back there. Ultimately, the judge didn't violate me, and my roommate and I completed our respective probations and skirted felony convictions.

The story comes full circle about 18 months later when I was subpoenaed to meet with the assistant district attorney to be interviewed again about the murder that happened the night before I was arrested. Apparently, they caught the suspected murderer, and I figured they were just re-interviewing everyone from back when it happened. It was interesting trying to explain to my boss why I had to dip out of work a couple of hours early. I waited in the lobby of the ADA's office in the Rolling Meadows courthouse and a younger dude starts chatting it up with me.

I told him, "I don't why I'm here, I'm no help. I told the cops I didn't see anything or whatever. I assume they are calling everybody in that they originally spoke to. You don't know shit, do ya?"

He straight up launched into a story about how his cousin had been staying in that apartment complex for a few months and right after the murder, he disappeared and left town.

He said, "When they called me in, I told the cops about my cousin disappearing. They bought me Portillo's, bro, and gave me a burner cell phone to call him so they could triangulate his position. They nabbed him and arrested him."

I was dumbfounded. "Are you fucking serious man?"

"Yeah, and they gave me $50 bucks, too."

"Dude, I know you said it's your cousin, but if you testify about all this shit, his people are gonna come after you, man. He may get life in prison for this, and you're like the key to the whole case."

Before we could finish the conversation, someone called his name, and he headed in to meet with the ADA. He was in there for a good 30 minutes and after talking to him, this shit was lock & key, closed shut case.

"Mr. Kubiak, turns out we won't need to meet with you today. We apologize for any inconvenience."

No shit, man, I thought. That dude is the only witness you need.

I left the courthouse that day grateful that everything related to the whole "horticulture" nonsense, and all the tangential bullshit, was now officially over. I was doubly grateful that I wasn't going to have to testify in open court and put my cousin behind bars for murder like that poor bastard.

That sort of seems like an anticlimactic ending to all the chaos that went down, but after that, I did steer clear of the illegal plant game... well, for a little while anyway.

5

2006 NFC Championship Game

Orchestrating toxic madness
Positioning oneself amidst the satirical redundancy
The righteousness of self-will encapsulating the suffering moments
Of fragile souls pacing through toxic courtyards.
Resistance subdued
Alluding to fictitious fallacies
Slowly discarding creativity for implausible defiance
Maintenance destroyed.

It was halftime of the Bears vs. Saints in the 2006 NFC Championship Game on January 21, 2007, and I had six or seven of my buddies at my apartment to watch the game. We were having a great time drinking and getting high. I decided to walk to the gas station nearby to pick up a pack of smokes. Less than 50 yards away, my phone rang, and it was Sophie, a former coworker whom I hadn't seen or heard from in at least a year.

I was all sorts of fucked up, with the Bears leading by nine and just 30 minutes away from heading to the Super Bowl. I did a double take, like, really, is Sophie calling me right now? At halftime of the Bears game? Or am I just so fucked up that I'm seeing double?

"Hey, what's up?"

I had no idea what she might want or if she had even meant to call me. And I vaguely recalled that she owed me a hundred bucks from when we were working together. I doubted she was calling about the money and thought perhaps she was looking for another loan.

I answered while I walked to grab said Newport's. She told me a long-winded story about growing up in Uganda. The details are a bit fuzzy at this point, but the gist of it was that she never knew her father and moved to the U.S. with her mother when she was around 13. She attended high school and college here in the States. She said her mother had been in the process of getting them citizenship, but she had died suddenly.

I was miles from sober and tried to follow along as I made my way to the gas station. What the fuck is this all about? Why the fuck is she telling me all this shit? Maybe things were rough, and she just needed someone to talk to? Whatever the reason, I listened, dropping the occasional "okay" or "mm-hmm."

Then she told me that she was living with her boyfriend, who was from London and was here on a green card and couldn't help her stay in the U.S. She called me to ask for a huge favor so she wouldn't have to return to Uganda. Then it hit me. Holy shit, she's asking me if I would help her become a citizen.

I joked, "Wait, dude. Sophie, did you just like, propose to me?'

"Um, well, yes."

I didn't even hesitate. "I got you. Or should I say, 'I do?' Dude, I've never planned on getting married and never wanted kids and shit. So yeah, no problem."

She was thrilled at how easily this all went down.

The long-ranging implications and logistics were not on my mind. I just figured that I was doing someone I know a solid. I'm good people and this was a totally selfless act, just a chill guy helping someone out. Even though I didn't ask for anything in return, this was like co-dependency on steroids. I was putting her needs ahead of my own and convincing myself it was all good. I acknowledge it was not the act of a mentally healthy individual. To be fair, she was pretty fine, and that might have played into my decision.

After a gratitude-laced thank you from Sophie where she said she was thrilled and uber-appreciative and thankful, she said she'd be in touch. We hung up. There I was, drunk, high, smoking a Newport and thinking to myself, holy fuck, that was crazy! I had just left to grab a pack of squares and I came back engaged.

As I entered the door to my place, I tried to figure out the most humorous way to mention what the fuck just went down. I blurted out, "Guess who just got engaged, fellas?"

I told them the story and, of course, they didn't believe me. They thought I was fucking around and on some straight bullshit. I was pleading with them, showing them the caller ID from my phone, but they were less interested in my supposed engagement than in the game, which was starting back up after halftime. I left it alone and didn't think too much of it. Were we going to have a ceremony and get married? I gave it less than a 50% chance of happening.

Well, fuck was I wrong. Within a week, Sophie called, and shit got real.

"I need you to meet me at the courthouse after work on Thursday at 4:30 p.m. so we can sign papers to get a marriage certificate filed. Then, once we do that…"

Honestly, I didn't hear a whole lot after that, and I didn't need to. Okay… well, this is actually happening.

She told me the tentative date for a quick courthouse ceremony. Her boyfriend would attend to take pictures and we would go over the other details on Thursday.

I hesitantly said, "Great, sounds good." And we hung up.

That's when the wheels in my mind started spinning and playing out all the implications and potential issues this could create for me.

Let's remember that I was on probation for "unlawful manufacturing and distribution of narcotics." Two months prior to my "engagement," a suburban drug task force had kicked in my front door and arrested my roommate and I, and thoroughly trashed our place with a search warrant in hand, drug-sniffing dogs, and the whole thing. Our case was still pending, and at that point, we were on pre-trial probation. The call had gone too quickly for me to mention this to my future wife during our matrimonial discussion.

Somehow, I convinced myself that my legal situation would not hinder the upcoming marriage. I showed up for the ceremony at the Rolling Meadows courthouse and found a goddamn fiesta going on. Dozens of Hispanic couples and their families and friends were waiting for their own courthouse weddings. Eventually, they called our names, and we headed into the courtroom. There was a table with a couple of people off to the side to do identity and document verification and the judge sat at the front in his seat.

Guess who was checking marriage certificates and paperwork that day? My goddamn probation officer Jennifer. Are you fucking kidding me?

She immediately knew what was going on and said, sarcastically, "Huh, Mr. Kubiak, this is a very interesting time for you to be getting married. So... what's your bride-to-be's name?"

"Jennifer, this is my fiancé, Sophia." She saw right through me but didn't hold up the proceedings.

If that wasn't enough, the judge was the same judge who was presiding over my case which was still in progress at that time.

This was getting real, and I was nervous. What would we do when he said, "I now pronounce you husband and wife?" We had no rings, and her boyfriend was there to take pictures as proof for a later date. Should we kiss? That would be weird as fuck. Especially with the boyfriend right there. If we don't do something, my P.O. is going to know this whole thing is a sham and the last thing I need is to fuck that up and end up with a felony conviction on my record. He finally got to that part and we kind of turned to one another and the best way I can describe the embrace was this super-awkward, Christian bro side-hug thing. As this was happening, I caught a quick glance of my P.O., Jennifer, and I can just see her shaking her head. The boyfriend snapped a few photos and the whole thing was done in less than 15 minutes. Cool. I still got the rest of my Saturday. Now what? What's married life like?

Before I took off, Sophie asked if it would be cool to have her bank statement mailed to my house to give the impression that we were living together. I'm like, yeah, cool, no problem.

Then she filled me in on details of the plan starting with, "Okay, so we need to stay married for at least two years, and then we can file for divorce, and I'll be eligible for citizenship and everybody wins."

Done. That works, man.

"Before we file for divorce, we're going to be interrogated separately by Immigration and Naturalization Service (INS) and the questions can get very specific. We'll have to know how many brothers and sisters each other has. What side of the bed did we sleep on? What are one another's middle names? What color is the phone in the house? Do you wear boxers or briefs?"

"Right. We'll cross that bridge when we come to it and make sure our stories are straight," I said. In my head, I was tripping out. I'm like, I'm already on probation and now I'm gonna be federally fucked if this whole thing goes south. I don't need this shit. I need to get high.

"Great, I'll be in touch."

We parted ways, and I smoked a blunt and stopped to grab a coffee somewhere in downtown Arlington Heights.

My mom called to say "Hi" and asked what I was up to.

"I just got married," I said, curious to hear what her reaction would be.

"Right..." She wasn't buying it.

"I'm serious."

"Whatever, Rob. You need to stop getting high."

Click.

During the next few weeks, Sophie's Citibank statements began arriving in the mail. I simply tossed them in a drawer and went about my life as if nothing happened. Once in a while, when I was fucked-up drinking and getting high with my buddies, I'd crack a joke about how I should probably call my wife. Or how the wifey probably wouldn't approve of me doing cocaine all night. I'm pretty sure none of them believed me and I can't blame them. I had zero proof of this happening, and no copy of a marriage certificate because she kept it. They'd never met her, so they couldn't ask her either and the idea was so far-fetched to begin with.

Not long after the "marriage," the landlord evicted me for not paying rent. Why would I pay rent when I could take my roommate's half and spend it on alcohol and drugs? By the end of the year, I would violate my probation for a dirty drop and take a brief four-day vacation to 26th and California and the Cook County Jail. Not long after that, I found myself at SHARE rehab in Hoffman Estates when my colleagues found out about a drug-fueled escapade I had with a coworker. During the next year or two, I was in and out of five different psych wards, detoxes, treatment centers, and the like.

No surprise that I lost touch with Sophie over the years. My phone number had changed several times, but she found me on Facebook and asked for my new number. I didn't respond. I did not want to deal with that shit right now. Then one time when I was high and bored and lonely, I sent her a direct message. I joked, "Hey Mrs. Kubiak, I feel like you may be cheating on me," because her Facebook posts included photos of her kid. Strangely enough, the father was not the bloke from London who took the pictures at our wedding. He was a guy from Uganda or somewhere in Africa or some shit.

A few more years passed with more rehabs for me, and another kid for her. We were way past the original plan of two years of marriage and then an amicable divorce, but I didn't care. If it was up to me, we could stay married forever; I had no plan or prospects for marriage. And frankly, the idea of an interrogation by INS was not something I wanted to sign up for.

In 2014, we had been married for seven freakin' years and I was balls deep in what I would describe as my quasi-functional heroin addiction. Sometimes I went to work, often nodding out at my desk in front of my computer, but it was enough to remain employed. She reached out one day and told me that she and the father of her children wanted to get married because they loved each other and wanted to make it official. Plus, the marriage would then allow him to obtain citizenship.

Obviously, we needed to get divorced first. I agreed to meet her after work at a bar in Oakbrook to sign some paperwork indicating that I was not contesting the divorce. Luckily, enough time had passed since the marriage that we didn't have to submit to an interrogation, and we could simply separate for amicable differences. Sweet. That settled my nerves.

The following week, we met up, and I met her future husband. A big win for me was that I finally got a photo of the original marriage certificate. Proof. Now I could convince people that I hadn't been making up a charade for the past seven years. I signed something, got my pic of the certificate and we parted ways. She mentioned that we'd have to meet at the courthouse to make it official and that she'd call me with the details.

A month or so later I heard from Sophie. She told me that if neither party contested the divorce, we wouldn't even need to go in front of a judge. She could fill out additional paperwork at the courthouse clerk's office and for a few hundred dollars in processing fees, they would issue a quicky divorce. She said that she would cover the processing fees.

"That sounds good. What do I need to do?"

"We just need to meet at the courthouse sometime this week and get it handled."

I thought, this sounds almost too good to be true, but I didn't look into it myself and said, "Sure."

I showed up, and she was there with one of her kids. What the fuck? Why would you bring one kid, who clearly isn't mine, and shows no signs of Caucasian-ness in her at all? Why didn't she leave this kid with the other one instead of dragging her into court? The whole thing seemed fucked. Whatever, I just wanted to get this over with.

Our number was called, and we approached the counter. The clerk reviewed our paperwork and said, "Okay, okay, okay, everything looks good and neither party is contesting it?"

"Correct."

"And your combined annual income is under $35,000?"

I paused, "No."

Sophie looked at me like, "What are you doing?"

With all the trouble I was in, the last thing I wanted was for the county to check my tax records and catch me lying about my income. Well, that killed the whole process.

With all the research she had done, how the fuck did she not know about the income stipulation? I was pissed to have taken a half day off work to meet her and for what?

She apologized for not doing her due diligence. "Well, the other option is to get a court date to make it 'official.' I'll get the details and be in touch. Probably means a higher fee."

"Okay, cool, yeah, just let me know."

In the seven years of marriage, I had only seen her in person a handful of times, which was indicative of the transactional nature of our relationship. Crazy.

A few months later, in 2015, she told me that she had paid the costs and secured a court date.

"Meet me at the courthouse at 1:00 p.m. next Thursday."

"Sure." I was looking forward to finally closing the book on this chapter of my life.

On Thursday, I was way too fucking high to walk into a courtroom and stand in front of a judge. Even if I had been sober that day, I didn't know how to properly explain to my boss that I needed to take the afternoon off to divorce my Ugandan wife. Shamefully, I turned my cell phone ringer off and ghosted her. She called and texted dozens of times.

I felt kind of bad, but the dope helped drown that out. Eventually, she stopped calling and I didn't know if she had pulled off the divorce without me.

Several years and rehabs later, I was in a group session at Banyan Treatment Center in Naperville. The counselor, Bonnie, asked, "Does anyone have any loose ends that they would like to tie up now that you're sober?"

"Yeah, Rob, 37, heroin... um, so like can your wife get like an absentee divorce if she can't find you and shit?"

A handful of my buddies chuckled. Knowing me and the fact that I had been to 18 rehabs before arriving at Banyan, there was no way they would believe I could be married.

Bonnie asked, "You're married?"

"Well, that's what I'm trying to figure out."

A few more chuckles.

"How do you not know?"

"Well, do you remember when the Bears went to Super Bowl in 2006?"

And then I proceeded to launch into the story I just described.

6

Library Evacuation

Formulating pretentious intentions and surrealistic normalcies
And parading through monotony at an alarming rate
Resurrecting subconscious desires between archaic stereotypes
With righteous indecision guiding this miscalculated journey
Breathing fire and lamenting forgone conclusions
Splendid variations of subliminal regret and undefined valor
Awash in the nothingness of transposed precision.

After I did another stint in a facility with 60 days of inpatient dual-diagnosis treatment and rehab, things were going off the rails at work. I had gone to rehab to keep my job, but it wasn't long before I was right back to using again. I was in a dark, dark place, struggling with the early stages of falling back into my heroin addiction. I just wanted to die. I was miserable, I hated my bullshit, pathetic existence and I was tired. I didn't care anymore. Even though I wanted to keep my job, that wasn't enough to keep me from using and I planned to just keep it under control.

That plan did not work. I was broke and clinging to my job for dear life. One day at work while taking a cigarette break with a coworker, I overshared how I was feeling. I found out later that she was concerned enough to talk to our Human Resources department about the conversation.

When I got home from work, I searched around in my roommate's closet and found a gun that he had accepted as collateral for some cocaine he fronted to one of my friends. Without hesitation, I put it in my coat, got in my car, and started driving. I figured it would be better for me to kill myself alone in my car, so my roommates wouldn't come home and find me dead in the apartment. That's probably not an image you could ever get out of your head.

People from work were texting me, and I turned my phone on silent. I didn't want to talk to them, but ironically, I wanted them to be concerned, to feel bad for me. It was incredibly self-indulgent. At one point, I replied to a text from a colleague and said that I was driving around with a handgun, and I didn't know what I was going to do. Bad idea.

I drove and drove and didn't know where to go. I ignored the calls and texts that were still coming in. After a while I stopped to try and collect my thoughts before I put the gun to my head and pulled the trigger to feel relief from everything. The Barrington Area Library was a familiar place, and I parked in the lot. I didn't want to bring the gun in with me, so I left it in the back seat and threw a small towel over it.

I sat in the lobby in a comfortable lounge chair and thought about what to do. I don't remember how long I sat there, but at some point, I glanced at my phone, and amidst the missed calls and texts, my buddy Justin had texted me. He also had a low-key heroin habit and was the only person that might have heroin that could make me feel better and allow me to escape.

I read his message and it said, "Dude, they triangulated your cell phone position and know you're at the library and have a gun. You gotta get out of there. I'll come get you."

Holy shit. What the fuck. I texted him back, "Come now."

"Already on my way, five minutes. Get the fuck out of there."

I jumped up and made a beeline for the front door. As I hurried, I took the battery out of my cell phone and transitioned from suicidal to terrified. Halfway down the sidewalk, two cop cars were pulling up to the front door. Justin was right behind them. I jumped in his car, and we got the fuck outta there.

He told me about the coworker who went to HR because she thought I would harm myself, and how they had notified the authorities as a safety measure. They were probably also covering themselves from legal liability if I did do something.

"What do you want to do?"

"Now? Heroin."

"Yep, I figured. I've got like 80 bucks. Wanna go down and see dude?"

I settled down a bit knowing that some heroin was on the way to save me.

We made our way to the West Side and copped some dope. As we talked, it became clear that the only way for me to protect my employment status would be for me to check myself into the hospital again. Fine. Once I had a couple of blows in me, I didn't care what the fuck I needed to do. Frankly, I was happy to just veg out for a while, go to some groups and leave the real world behind for as long as they would keep me.

Once we got right from the dope, we headed back to the suburbs so I could get my car and drive myself to a hospital or treatment center. We approached the library on Northwest Highway, and just as we were about to turn in, we saw that the parking lot was empty, except for my car which was getting hauled onto a flatbed pickup truck.

Fuuuuuuck. What the fuck, man? How did they know that was my car and why was it getting towed? I probably could have figured that out if I had been sober, but I wasn't. We were both totally fucked up. Later, I learned that the cops notified the library about someone with a gun and told them to evacuate for safety measures. Everyone else drove off, leaving my car alone in the parking lot.

Without a car and unsure whether I could get a bed in a psychiatric hospital, I didn't know what to do. Justin didn't either. Mostly, Justin just wanted to get home and leave the problem to me so he could keep his habit under wraps.

My mom's house wasn't too far from the library, and I found myself calling her from Justin's phone.

"Mom, it's Rob. I think I need to go to the hospital. Can you drive me?"

"Again? Do you feel like you're going to hurt yourself?"

"I do."

"Okay, fine. Come over and I'll take you somewhere."

She knew I had been dabbling in heroin for a while, but when Justin dropped me off and she saw how fucked up I was, there was no more hesitation. She got me right over to Alexian Brothers in Hoffman Estates, and I was initially admitted to the psych unit.

Having been in and out of psych units and rehabs so many times, once the initial shock of being admitted wore off, I acclimated easily and found a satisfying comfort in the place. It felt like a vacation from reality, which was what I was trying to do with drugs in the first place. No phone. No visits. No collection calls or voicemails. No work. My only responsibility was to make my bed and attend groups. Sure, you couldn't have a belt or shoelaces or smoke, but it was a small tradeoff for the stress-free environment.

When I arrived, I first met my new roommate. He was about eight years younger and struggling with the same issues I had—he also was developing his own low-key heroin habit. We got along famously. He and I exchanged contact info with the full intention of hanging out and getting fucked up together after we were released.

Somewhere between grabbing the gun out of the closet and the end of my time at Alexian, I lost the overwhelming desire to die. Maybe it was the meds, the treatment, the people, I don't know, but it dissipated.

Once we got out, we started hanging out. We copped some dope from his connection, a few blocks from Leamington Foods. We started drinking, smoking weed, doing coke, and eating pills on weekends as if nothing had ever happened. He started taking Xanax that he bought from my roommate, and he was over at my place all the time for the next couple of months.

At one point, I asked my roommate to stop selling him so many Xanax bars because he was getting way too fucked up. One night, I watched him take a half-hour to back his Jeep Cherokee out of the parking lot. He was blacking out a lot and eating 2mg bars by the handful. It wasn't good, but honestly, who was I to tell anyone what to do with their drugs?

One Thursday night, we decided to have a party. We grabbed a keg and invited a bunch of people over. My buddy and I ran some errands, picking up smokes, and getting some coke and pills. He saw me take my Suboxone, which is prescribed to suppress the urge for heroin, and he asked if he could have a couple.

"Dude, I don't think it's gonna do anything but yeah, if you want."

"Cool."

"Here man, just let them dissolve in your mouth."

We got home, did a bunch of coke, and were just getting fucked up and hanging out with everyone. The party started to wind down around 2:00 a.m. He asked if he could crash at our place because he didn't want to drive home. No problem.

I had to work the next day, so we tried to get some sleep. He asked if I could set the alarm for 7:30 a.m. when I left for work so he could get up and meet his grandma for breakfast. Yeah, for sure.

We talked a bit and made plans to catch a Cubs game together. He told me someone in his family, a grandfather or somebody, worked for or was part owner of either the Pittsburgh Pirates or the Brewers, I forget which, but he said he could probably get us free box seats. Sweet, man, that would be dope. Yeah.

I was so wired that falling asleep was probably futile, but I tried. I heard him, on the opposite side of the air mattress, start to snore. How the fuck is he able to doze off like that? Fuckin' Xanax man. Whatever, he wasn't driving, so I thought it was fine.

By 6:30 a.m. when the alarm went off, I hadn't had more than 30 minutes of shuteye. I reset it to 7:30 a.m. as he'd asked. I showered and tried to tell him that I was taking off, but he was out.

Somewhere between leaving my room and getting into my car, I realized that I was in no condition to go to work and called in sick. I texted my good buddy Justin, on the off chance that he was still up partying, and sure enough, he was. He told me to come through, so rather than taking Lake Cook Road toward my office, I stopped at Country Glen, where he was living with his girlfriend Lisa, just a mile or so away.

I was glad they were still up doing coke and fucking around. I knew I could rely on him. He was probably the only friend I had that drank and drugged the way that I did. Shortly after I got there, my roommate called. What the fuck does he want? As far as he knows, I'm at work, man.

"Dude, your alarm keeps going off."

"Yeah, it's for my man. He's going to breakfast with his grandma. Just go turn it off and wake him up, man."

"I tried, dude, but he's not breathing. I think he's dead."

"Shut the fuck up man, what do you really need, bro?"

"I'm serious. He's like blue and like dead. You need to come over here. Where are you?"

"I'm near my work," which was a lie. I was six blocks away at Justin's.

"Well, you need to come back here, man. For real, dude, come home."

"Fine, but if he's okay I'm gonna fucking kill you, man."

"Okay, just get over here."

I relayed this shit to Justin and Lisa, and none of us believed he was for real. Justin agreed to come with me while Lisa stayed behind, and we headed back to my place, all tweaked out. We walked in and found Craig and one of his buddies, John, frantic.

"Dude, he's blue and not breathing."

Justin and I headed into my room and holy shit, they weren't just fucking with us. He looked dead. He is dead. John was freaking out and trying to do CPR and Justin and I said, "Bro, he's gone."

I'm in no way a medical expert and don't know whether or not there was anything we could have done to save him. He couldn't have been that way for long because I left just over an hour ago and he did not look like that. There was dried vomit on his cheek and on the carpet beside the air mattress.

We all panicked. There were drugs and paraphernalia scattered all over the house and we were more worried about that than whether there was anything we can do to help him.

These days, with the Good Samaritan law, you can call an ambulance for an overdose or drug-related incident without fear of repercussions for drugs in your possession and your own involvement. But at that time, calling an ambulance meant the cops would show up and they would probably arrest us. Plus, none of us were in any condition to talk to the authorities. What the fuck do we do?

His car was parked out front.

"What if we get him into his car, drive it to the Menards up the street, and leave him there in the driver's seat?"

"Yes."

"Yes. That's what we need to do. Just get him the fuck out of here."

Lisa called. "What the fuck is taking so long?"

"Dude is legit dead."

"Fuck you guys."

"No, seriously, he is done."

"Fuck you. I'm coming over there and if he's not dead I'm gonna kill you guys."

"Fine."

We decided to wait for Lisa. Maybe she could help us get him out of here.

She walked into the bedroom. "He's not breathing, did you call 9-1-1?"

"No man, there's nothing they can do."

"How the fuck do you know?"

She started to dial, and I knocked the phone out of her hand.

"What are you doing?"

"If you call, we will all be arrested," I said. "Look around, you can't call the paramedics."

"He's gonna die if we don't."

Justin said, calmly, "Babe, he's already dead."

"Yeah, Lisa, we just need to get him out of here now."

"WHAT?"

We explained the plan.

"Are you fucking serious? Are you listening to yourselves right now? You'll be locked up forever if you do that."

"Well, do you have a better plan?"

"Yes, we need to call an ambulance."

Thank God Lisa came over because she was right. If we had carried out our plan, we would all be in prison to this day.

Eventually, we agreed that my roommate along with his buddy John, who had both gotten some sleep and had most of their wits about them, would hide the drugs and paraphernalia and call the ambulance. Lisa,

Justin, and I would go back to their apartment to keep doing cocaine. Once the ambulance had come and gone and everything was sorted out, they would shoot us a text and join us. None of us wanted to stay there with a dead body, but somehow Craig and John agreed to the plan.

Less than an hour later, Craig called. "It's over. He's gone. They took him away and everything's cool. We're coming by."

Within 30 minutes or so, we had an unspoken agreement that we were not going to talk about what just happened. It was on everyone's mind, but continuing to mull over the events of that night and morning was not going to change the outcome. We went on a three-day cocaine bender and did our best to escape reality. We powered through and hid from the emotions and fucked-up-ed-ness of it all. Eventually, we came down late Sunday, and things kind of returned to normal.

One of the grimiest feelings I've ever experienced was that Sunday evening when I returned to my room and found that my buddy was still logged in to his Gmail account on my laptop. I saw an email at the top of his inbox that was from his father. It was basically titled, *"A letter to my dead son."* I read the email and his dad said all the things he had wanted to say to him but never got around to. I honestly was so out of my mind that I don't remember a word of it, but I still feel horrible about myself for even eyeing that private message that was absolutely none of my business.

Just like after the robbery in college, I started getting voicemails from a detective who wanted to talk to me about the incident. They got the number for my work phone, and I picked it up, not knowing it was them. They told me they just needed me to come by the station.

"Okay, yeah, I'll stop by when I can." Fuck that. I had zero intention of going to the police station. Did they think I was stupid? There is no way that would turn out well for me. Perhaps the toxicology report showed that he had Suboxone in his system, along with the alcohol, cocaine, and beer that I bought. Plus, Benzo's from the Xanax my roommate provided him. Could we be charged with his death?

His mother left me a voicemail and it was clear that his family thought he had taken his own life. They thought that he must have just been so miserable, I mean we did meet at a psychiatric unit, that he just ingested all of those substances on purpose to kill himself. That was so far from the truth. He was happy almost all the time, and we were making plans to go to the Cubs game. It was a complete accident. We were just getting fucked up, enjoying ourselves, and it was a total accident. Holy shit. I was the only one that knew otherwise. I should have told them. I should have picked up the phone and called her and explained this to her. I couldn't. I couldn't even bring myself to attend the funeral.

Over the years, I occasionally get a friend request or message on social media from his mother, and I continue to ignore them. I changed my number and blocked her on Facebook. I was always struggling with my own issues, never able to provide clarity for them.

That was more than a decade ago. I know that even after all this time, I should call the family and explain the situation to them. I owe them at least that much. But 10 years later, I still can't summon the courage to do that.

After these past five years of sobriety and my work in a solid recovery program, I am probably in a position to offer amends and provide insight into his last moments. But whenever the topic comes up with my sponsor or others in the program, my first question is always, what's the statute of limitations on involuntary manslaughter?

7

Madden-ing

Hours creep forward drastically slow
The misguided and misunderstood
The arduous task of rehabilitation floats across the horizon
I gaze west with fiery eyes and all I see is a transparent glare.
Mundane surroundings make this so painstakingly slow
The lack of mental stimulation is almost enough to drive you mad
Recapitulating the same routine most of us have been stuck in for
years
Retreating into the scariest place imaginable – your cognition.

The next three years from 2009-12 were a living hell. I desperately wished I would just die and never wake up, nothing gave me enjoyment – utter anhedonia and towards the end, I was losing my mind. During that time I did and I experienced all the chaotic dope fiend antics – ODing, friends ODing in front of me and dying, popping up ashtrays in public places looking for cigarette butts, driving an hour and a half to grab one bag to split with a friend because we only had ten dollars, waiting an hour for my guy who kept saying he was right around the corner and would be there any minute, seeing J&J Fish restaurants every day, tying off in the car using my seatbelt, using Newport filters in lieu of cotton, sharting myself and peeing out of my asshole for days dope sick as fuck – all of it – any junkie knows what I'm talking about.

It all came to a head on Thursday morning, just after 10am on July 12th, 2012, and I have the day off work. I'm dope sick, I have no cigarettes. No food and no money. The 'check engine' light on my car went on a few days prior, and I don't get paid again for another week. I hate my predicament, my life, and myself. What am I going to do to avoid completely losing my mind worrying about everything? Then it occurs to me. Pawn some shit and go down and grab one. So, I throw my flat-screen television in the backseat of my car and ride on up to the pawn shop. Well, it turns out from all the wear and tear I put on my TV from previous pawning adventures, they can only offer me $28. Fuck man, that's two bags and a pack of Newport's and that's it. But of course, I do it anyway.

I holler at my man Ron, who is more commonly referred to by his street name of 'Green Eyes' out on the West Side. Ron is a light-skinned black dude, probably in his mid-50s at the time who is a lifelong dope fiend. Only snorts, never shoots, and probably hasn't been gainfully em-ployed in over thirty-five years (if ever). Each day we plotted, schemed, and figured out a way to get one more. He was a clever, MacGyver-esque dope fiend. If somebody needed their cable turned on, their oil changed, to figure out where to get some good weed - anything that could potentially land us a few bucks for the effort, he knew how to do it or where to get it. He always managed to figure out a way to get one more and always knew which spot had the best dope out on the West Side each day of the week.

I holler at Ron, "What's up man? What you up to?"

"Shiiiiiiiiiiiiit.....I need a blow Jack!"

I chuckle a bit. "I just pawned my tv, and 'bout to get some squares and I'll have a dub left, that'll at least get us a couple."

"Slide through bro."

And out West I go. I do a bag; he does the other and now that we've both got one in us, we can finally think straight, and we start scheming on how to get one more. As we're marinating ideas, I start describing how miserable I've been and that I'm ready and willing to just walk away from my life, and he kind of already knows that I'm not in a good place and down for whatever.

Before long, we're riding an hour and a half back to my place to facilitate me leaving my entire life behind and getting more money for dope in the process. We get back to my place and we load my laptop, my air conditioner, and a small duffel bag of clothes and toiletries into my car. I leave the house keys on the counter of the place I was renting from and vow never to return to that apartment. At that moment, I just decided that I was done, that this was it for me. I was going to walk away from my life, and I left all of my other things there – clothes, CDs, furniture, etc.

We then head an hour and a half back to the West Side and stop at a pawn shop down there. We sell the barely used $400 A/C unit to some Latino guy in the parking lot for $75. Then we go inside with the laptop, which I need to perform my job, and end up pawing that for $50. We go grab a half jab (6 bags of heroin) and a bite to eat from Sharks and head back to his sister's place. We eat the food, toot the blows, and run to the gas station. As we're getting back, parking out in the street, this guy that lives in the place across the street pulls in behind us.

"Hey homie, yo, you trying to sell your car?"

"Sure, make me an offer."

"Shit, what about $1,500?"

Now my car's easily worth $3,500-$4,000 at a bare minimum, but I'm like,

"Cool."

"Well, there are some scratches & whatnot. The most I can probably do is like $800."

"Oh, ok, whatever."

At this point, it becomes readily apparent to him that he's negotiating with a junkie that's high out of his mind. Eventually, I sell it for $400. He only had $350 on him, so technically that dude still owes me $50. I'm not sure why, but I then give all the money to Ron. I tell him to grab us a jab and that he can keep the rest. This was it for me. One last hurrah and then I had no idea what I was going to do.

Initially, he hesitates, but ultimately agrees to take it. At this point I no longer have my apartment, my car, or any money, and I don't have most of my possessions, including my laptop, which I needed for work. I didn't care. I was through. I had methodically gotten rid of almost every piece of my life over the course of about four hours. I was just giving up.

After my man returns with the jab, we get sufficiently high, and he tells me I can just crash there. Perfect – that saved me from having to ask and I didn't have any other options at that point. It's getting late and I decide I want to go up to the Walmart up on North Avenue. It's July 12th and even though it's like 9 pm, it's still like a sweltering 95 degrees, so, needless to say, it was a solo mission. I finally get up there and I'm sweating balls, I got dry mouth, a nasty case of swamp ass, and I think everyone is staring at me 'cuz I'm so faded. I quickly snatch up some soda and candy and make my way up outta there. I'm walking back, chain-smoking, and guzzling warm grape Crush straight out of the two-liter bottle. It's kinda nasty, but I'm dying of thirst. Eventually, I get back and my man politely informs me that he's a little concerned about me. I chuckle.

"Yeah, me too brother."

"No, for real."

"Yeah, I know," and he kind of expresses a more solemn look, and I'm like, "I don't know what the fuck I'm gonna do man."

"Exactly." Then he paused for a moment.

"Bro, I think you need to get some help and check yourself into the hospital."

"Uh, I don't really know about that man."

"What other options do you have?"

"I don't know.....Yeah, I guess you're right, but they won't admit me."

"Get creative."

I knew what that meant. I just had to tell them I want to hurt myself. Done that before, shit, I'll do it again. Around 5 am we hopped in his car, and I cut all ties to my former existence. First, I send a cryptic email to my employer from my cell phone saying something along the lines of, "*having serious personal problems and I am admitting myself to the hospital. I'm sorry, but I will need to resign and best of luck to you all going forward.*" So now I no longer have a job and as they are admitting me to Loretto Hospital, I give my cell phone to him to hang onto so I can just call my own number if I needed to contact him.

They put me in a room and I'm not entirely sure what the procedure is since this is the first time I've been in this predicament without health insurance. The instant I started to sense dope sickness setting in and realized they weren't going to give me anything for it I considered walking out of there, however, the uniformed CPD officer outside my room was enough of a deterrent to keep me from attempting that. Frustration set in.

I'm thinking, how fucking long are they gonna keep me here? It's been 24 hours already. I'm sick as hell and nobody is explaining anything to me. Eventually, this Filipino nurse came in and said, "Good news son, they accepted you at Madden." I presumed that it was some sort of state-funded mental health hospital, which is precisely what it turned out to be. I finally get transferred there via ambulance and I get to intake, extremely dope sick and this was a far cry from the various country-club-esque facilities out in the suburbs that I was accustomed to. It was a culture shock for me. All the nurses were mean and shit and they wouldn't even give me a blanket or a pillow. I asked three different nurses if I could just lay down somewhere before one told me that that would be okay.

I felt like shit, I knew I couldn't leave, and I thought, now I really done fucked up. I didn't realize they were going to transfer me to one of the units, which turned out to be quite similar to the aforementioned facilities I described, and I experienced some minimal relief. It turned out that I would be housed in Pavilion 2, Room 106 and it was there that I went through the final days of my dope sickness with a little help from the medications they began giving me.

Like I generally tend to do when I'm first admitted to mental health hospitals, I didn't leave my room for 2-3 days. Not even to eat or wash up. Then, slowly, I manage to slither out for a meal a day, then perhaps two, before I get acclimated. I declined to speak to any of the doctors or counselors for the first 5-6 days or so, and then I came around and enrolled in the program. I know at first, I was quite irritable. I was skipping all the groups that were offered and I was becoming righteously bored and soberer and soberer, which was the bigger problem.

I slowly started talking to the doctors and nurses, and taking the medications they prescribed. Eventually, I started spending more and more time outside my bed and in the dayroom. I wasn't interacting with any of the other clients and despite their very limited resources, I somehow managed to get an empty, dog-eared, and coverless composition notebook and a red BIC pen from one of the technicians. Off I went scribbling in the book like I always seem to do when I'm in treatment facilities. Initially, I was nervous to transcribe my thoughts and journal outside of my room, but eventually, I managed to get comfortable enough to journal out in the dayroom.

I got to work right away with some introspective explorations. I pushed myself to depths I'd previously left dormant and unexplored. Before long, everyone knew me as the white guy that was always writing. That was perfectly fine with me. I felt a remote connectedness to a handful of other people in my Pavilion who would pop over and admire my handwriting. (NOTE: I get this on a weekly basis to this day. I have the most impeccable tiny print, and am always journaling and it's so neat, clean, and perfect that people think it was printed off a computer, so I'm used to it.)

All I had was time and my mind was all over the place and I was not in the best of headspaces as you can probably tell from some of the early passages from that notebook:

At some point, I took a wrong turn and since then a wedge continues to be driven between the person I thought I was and the devoid caricature I've become.

It's hard to forget about past mistakes when you're still paying for them in the present.

I mean what really gives my life meaning and what makes me happy – right now I would say heroin, plain and simple and without question.

I think I do have a strong tendency to distance myself from the vulnerability that comes from things like love or success in life as well as the commitment that comes from family and friends. To such an extent that I've resigned myself to endure I live a life of perpetual loneliness.

I just don't have that persistent willingness to exert effort to help myself which has been identified as the most crucial predictor of recovery.

Am I giving up or giving in?

Not that they could fix everything, but sometimes all you need is someone to fix anything.

Shared experiences. Personal relationships. I should have listened to that sage advice back in 1999, about how most of what is important is invisible to the eye.

I really do feel cornered by life.

Excuses come a lot cheaper than reasons these days.

I'm sick of feeling like I'm always gonna be fixing things for the rest of my life.

To be completely honest, after a while, I began to get nervous about appearing to be getting better, because I had nothing left and nowhere to go once I was discharged. I tried to suppress any feelings of joy or outward expressions of happiness. Hold up. Who am I kidding? For the first month I was there I wanted to leave, grab two jabs, prepare ten shots, bang 'em all one after another, and hope to never wake up. I didn't know whether that would work out, but slowly the constant feelings of worthlessness began to dissipate. I still didn't want to be discharged, but I started working productively with the staff. I don't know, but perhaps because of how bad my depression was, they didn't push me to try and figure out where to go from there. They also performed several psychological tests on me for one reason or another and that allotted me some additional time there.

I started getting very comfortable with it all and while the average stay was rarely ever more than 5-7 days, I would end up being there for 59 days before I was finally emancipated. During the course of my stay, I began to acclimate and embrace the place. I even won the inpatient talent show they did with the clients. Twice actually, because I was there for so goddamn long. (NOTE: Refer to Appendix I to view one of those winning spoken word/free verses I performed in its entirety).

At one point I remember thinking to myself, if they told me that I was going to have to spend the rest of my life at Madden, I would have been just fine with it. I felt safe and okay there. There wasn't much expected of you, and it was a lot less terrifying than having to start over again out in the real world.

During my stay, I became decent associates with one of the other patients in my pavilion. He was there for almost a month himself and he seemed to make a concerted effort to help convince me that hey, why not go to treatment when I'm discharged instead of going back out West and continuing to drink & drug myself into oblivion? It seemed like every day he kept driving on me about it too. Since we were partners in the art of secretly smoking squares in the bathroom.

Yeah, you had to kind of slyly disappear, and take turns standing on the toilet, holding the cigarette up near the vent so as not to get caught. Because of that aspect alone, he had my undivided attention quite a bit more than anyone else in the place, and what he was saying started to rub off on me. Even one of the technicians began driving on me about giving treatment another try. I had nothing to go back to anyway and at the minimum, it would give me 28 more days to loiter around until I ultimately needed to make up my mind as to where to go and what to do. I could handle that I suppose. I've always enjoyed my previous treatment experiences and have generally gotten along quite well with other recovering addicts.

Essentially, two weeks after my new associate had left for treatment, I followed and went to the same facility. As soon as I was admitted I knew I had made the right decision and I knew four other guys that were in the same Pavilion with me at Madden. It made the transition that much smoother, and I started feeling progressively more content with each passing day. I had been journaling voraciously for two months at Madden and I explored every introspective possibility at that point. On my second day at South Suburban Treatment Center, it finally occurred to me. I had been struggling to develop a premise for a book or film for years. I had been wanting to do that for the past decade or so but would always find myself jotting down mediocre fiction that never really went anywhere and I would eventually just get frustrated and give up. I finally felt inspired to write something for the first time in a long time and I had some direction.

So, thirteen years after the fact, on the golden anniversary of my wrist-slitting incident, I began scribbling down my first attempt at telling my 'story'. It would still take another ten years, including another half decade of pain and suffering before I'd be in a position to tell my story and publish the original *rob 37 heroin* along with this book, both of which include tidbits and passages from that original effort.

It was hand-written in five notebooks over the course of the next seventy-seven days, finally finishing it on December 1, 2012. The following day, December 2nd, 2012, was the first time I was ever asked to speak at an AA or NA meeting. It was at the Sunday 10:15 am speaker meeting at the Harvey 100 Club. What was a white dude like me doing in Harvey? Two words: Belle Court.

Once I was discharged, I landed at a halfway/three-quarter house in Phoenix, IL (a tiny town next to Harvey in Thornton Township) at a place called Belle Court. It was a two-story house, with two apartments, both of which had 3 bedrooms and there were 5 of us per apartment. Two double rooms and the house manager for each had their own private bedroom. I was one of maybe eight white people in Harvey and I arrived there with around sixty days sober. It was all sorts of fucked up at first and challenging for me to navigate and figure out how to operate. There was a large recovery community, and they embraced my newly sober ass, and I quickly became affectionately known as 'White Rob' 'round the rooms.

I got clean/sober for what would ultimately be almost two years by going to meetings daily at the Harvey 100 club. I don't know if any of you have ever been to a meeting there, but I assure you it's nothing like the meetings out in Naperville or Westmont. I was giving leads, chairing meetings, I was fucking plugged in, but I wasn't honestly working steps and didn't exactly have a sponsor.

Then I moved out (more like kicked out) of Harvey and Belle Court and the whole relapse cliché started playing itself out. I detached from my recovery community and wasn't working steps. I stopped going to meetings and got busy at work. I was just white-knuckling it and was fucking miserable. Just as miserable, if not more, than at the tail end of my using days.

Eventually, a had a few drinks at a company party. Then, a month or so later, I started smoking weed and as the story goes, within three months I was back using heroin. I began almost immediately using all day, every day, going to work and trying to convince myself I was a 'functional junkie'.

Honestly, have you ever met a 'functional junkie'?

Yeah, me neither.

8

Conclusion

I'm approaching my five-year anniversary of being clean and sober and it's been almost a year since I finished transcribing the original (the O.G.) *rob 37 heroin*. As I finish this book, I realize how far I've come. I clearly remember sitting in what I hope will be my last rehab back in September of 2017 and daydreaming about the future. I was thinking of best-case scenarios for myself. I was a homeless, unemployed 37-year-old heroin addict in my nineteenth treatment center. If everything imaginable worked out for me going forward, what could life look like?

Don't we all periodically conjure up an image in our head of what life could look like? Maybe you imagine you have a really good job making six figures and a nice car. Perhaps your future self owns a condo or a home with a white picket fence and is on track to retire early. Or maybe you dream you're married or have a significant other and some kids. Whatever that idyllic vision is for you.

In September 2017, entering rehab AGAIN, I did the math and had a rudimentary best-case scenario of what life could be for me. I'm not going to get into specifics, but I would describe it as "settling." I was perfectly okay with settling for a less-than-desirable future for myself. I was convinced that my past transgressions made the odds stacked against me and I was signing up to live a 70% version of my life. I figured that the other 30% echelon was not in the cards for me, and I settled on a modest ideation of my life. Had I not done x-y-and-z or fucked things up for almost two decades, or been a full-blown junkie, I could have been successful or lived out the life I dreamed about as a child.

But, at about the 18-month mark in recovery, I realized I had achieved everything in my "settling" vision. It wasn't like one day I woke up and realized I'd accomplished all these things, it just occurred to me over time. Holy shit I thought – we did it. And the amazing thing is that I didn't default to my standard operating mode and choose comfort over character-building. This time I didn't take my foot off the accelerator and start to coast. I wanted to see if I could continue moving the needle forward.

I was ascending into that implausible 30% realm and realized that so much more was possible. That being an addict in recovery was not a life-limiting proposition. For the first time I honestly, like deep down inside me, truly believed that there were endless possibilities. I also understood that it meant doing more. That what got us "here" was not going to get us "there." I had established a solid routine that helped me get to where I was, but I had to continue growing and bettering myself and reset the bar.

Exercising daily. Fixing your shitty credit score. Asking for a raise at work. Finishing school or getting that degree. Traveling to another country. Spending more time with the kids. Writing a book. Whatever the fuck it is for you, it all starts with changing our daily habits. Trying new things and daring to fail. Pushing ourselves outside our comfort zone. Identifying a short- or long-term goal and accomplishing it. Surrounding ourselves with people who celebrate and appreciate us. All these things are small steps in the right direction and moving us to that next tier.

It took action. It took effort. Whenever I'm stuck, whether it's in a bad headspace during the day, trying to decide whether I should go back to school or change jobs, or even if I'm just unsure what to do with myself on a Sunday afternoon with a few hours of free time. I've learned that for me, **action is always the antidote.** Sitting around ruminating about problems or laying on the couch never gets me anywhere. Once I start making some moves and putting myself out into the world—things materialize. Opportunities present themselves.

Having lengthy conversations with myself in my head and trying to sort things out in my life or the world's problems never gets me anywhere. And generally, I end up beating myself up later for not accomplishing anything. Nobody judges us harsher than we judge ourselves, right? Like, if another human being spoke to me the way I talk to myself, with all the negative self-talk and whatnot, I would never hang out with that person. We're our own worst critics. Quickly taking some action. Helping somebody. Taking a spontaneous field trip. Trying something new. Anything else is always better for me.

I've shared my story because if I leave you with anything, I'd like to think it's some hope. Perhaps some motivation. What happened to you before this moment is irrelevant. You are not defined by what's inside your head. You are what you do. Be bold. Take action. Remember, we are all one decision away from a completely different life so make it a good one. Find your purpose and get out there and make some memories.

My actual Madden Mental Health talent show winning free verse/poem I performed for my unprecedented second talent show win. I landed a six-pack of Reese's peanut butter cups for winning, which were like gold at that place.

(Originally written on the afternoon of 8/11/2012)

It's twilight - not my light.
For my light don't shine in glorious rays
Instead, it's spent thinking about better days
In a haze of blunt smoke and lookin' for a fix
Things done changed when dope came in the mix
Transfixed on searching for that metaphorical vein
What started off as fun, would barely ease the pain
Insane is what became of this prodigal son
Snorting and shooting until I was numb
Dumb? Yeah, looking back you can see
4am sick on the corner, yeah that was me
Eternity is what I spent, both time and money
When I couldn't cop, my nose would get runny
Funny? No fuckin' way
And too many people had to pay
And to this day I will still never regain that trust
I'm certainly lucky that I never got bust....
-ed, I tried to rid myself of all the pain & sorrow
And focus on the promise of a brighter tomorrow
Borrow? Yeah, wherever and whenever I could
I restored to stealing, even that I knew I should
Not grab that jab and cook up that shot
Unsure where I was going, but nowhere's where I got
Not ready for the emotional turmoil
All it did was cause my integrity to spoil
Foil? Yeah, I quickly unroll that shit

And dump out that powder and get ready for a hit
Quit? Why would I, I'm homeless and broke
And even to the $5 dollar trick, I'm the joke
Smoke? Yeah, and it to the dome it all went
Spent every waking hour just trying to get bent
Saying things I shouldn't, just trying to vent
But once I got high, I knew what I meant
Heaven sent, is hopefully where I'm headed
Into your consciousness is where I hope this gets embedded
Regret it? Yeah, from time to time
But at least I'm still here to finish this rhyme
Flatline.

During the course of finalizing the last of the book edits and it going to print, I celebrated five years of sobriety/clean time on September 8, 2022. Just wanted to share another heroin cake-baking masterpiece from my buddy Dan. His heroin cakes get more and more delicious each year!

About the Author

After nearly twenty years of struggling with addiction, spending a good chunk of his adult life in miscellaneous treatment centers, psych units, detoxes, hospitals, and ICUs, Rob managed to get his life together. He's been clean and in recovery for over five years now and it's something he has become incredibly passionate about and enjoys working with others. He can regularly be found scribbling in his journal with impeccable handwriting that almost looks like it was computer-generated. *Making Girls Cry Since '79* is his self-proclaimed tagline and online dating profile header. He thoroughly enjoys candies and sweets of all kinds with a perhaps unhealthy predilection for HI-CHEW's and Haribo gummies. His childhood tv crush was Christine Lakin who played Alicia 'Al' Lambert on *Step by Step*, part of ABC's classic TGIF Friday lineup in the early '90s. Also claims he has not eaten a fruit or vegetable since the early '90s, and well...we believe him. Loves PB&J on saltines, prefers sorbet to traditional ice cream, and never drinks the milk at the bottom of his bowl of cereal. He currently resides in the greater Chicagoland area, is active in the recovery community, and is also the author of the iconic *rob 37 heroin*.